VEGAN VEGAN!

VEGAN VEGAN!

ZIZI
HATTAB

Φ

Gluten-free Nut-free Less than 30 minutes 5 or fewer ingredients

I

INTRODUCTION

Foreword by Joan Roca

When Zizi decided to open her first restaurant in 2020, she chose to make it 100 per cent vegan. Many feared for her future. It was the kind of daring and bold choice that made people ask, "Have you lost your mind?"

Opening a business aimed at a minority market was already risky. Doing so while completely rethinking the foundations of one's entire culinary training demanded an almost reckless ingenuity. My brother Josep and I were confronted with similar doubts in the 1980s when we had the idea of opening our first modern restaurant. "Who's going to come? Have you gone mad?" Yes—it was more heart than head, but our lives changed the day we opened our door for business.

Intuition is an art of living. And it stands behind the most brilliant decisions. One should never contradict a gut feeling. Intuition drove Zizi to leave her successful engineering career in Zurich. She embarked on a five-year journey without guarantees, worked in some of the best restaurants in the world, and learned directly in their kitchens what her great mind had absorbed during long nights reading cookbooks in her tiny Zurich apartment.

As of the day I write these lines, only one woman in the world holds a Michelin star for a purely plant-based restaurant: Zizi. She does not proclaim it. Humility, after all, is a trait most often found in true leaders, in and out of the kitchen.

Zizi's intelligence and wit shone when she worked in my kitchen as a stagiaire. Zizi is a chef of undeniable talent, but she also has a privileged emotional intelligence. I believe she will be one of the leading voices in the humanist culinary revolution that is still taking shape. To look at the world through the heart requires great courage—and Zizi has no shortage of guts; she has proven it.

Zizi still has much cooking to do and much to say. And I feel fortunate to have the space to continue telling the stories of a talented chef whom I admire deeply and hold in great affection—of Zizi, who is an example of tenacity, passion, humility, heart, and intellect.

Joan Roca

Preface

My name is Zineb Hattab, but everyone calls me Zizi. Cooking with plants opened my eyes to an entirely new world of flavors and possibilities, challenging everything I thought I understood about food and cooking. I spent years working in some of the world's most demanding kitchens: handling whole animals at Blue Hill, spending endless hours butchering at Osteria Francescana, and breaking down fish at Cosme. None of the skills I learned prepared me for the path I was about to take—at least not in the way I expected.

What mattered most turned out to be the work I had once overlooked. I spent nearly a full day every week juicing cherries at one restaurant and scraping the insides of fava (broad) bean pods at another. Elsewhere, I picked twenty-four varieties of herbs and flowers daily for salads and cut diamond-shaped apples until my fingertips were raw. Now, cooking plants with love is what we do every day at my restaurants.

My mission is to elevate plant-based cooking to the highest level and to normalize the care we bring to our food choices. That shift changed the way I cook—and the way I think about food—entirely. And with *Vegan Vegan!*, my goal is to make plant-based cooking easy and approachable. Here, you'll find delicious adaptations of beloved dishes at my restaurants, such as the Grilled Salad (page 138) or Roasted Carrots with Labneh and Kikos (page 161). I will show you how to build flavor confidently (page 15) and how to stock your pantry with essential mayos, spice blends, and sauces to coax the most from your ingredients and make your food sing with flavor (page 253).

Vegan Vegan! is about commitment—choosing to cook with plants fully, confidently, and with pleasure. I love to capture the abundance of vegetables, grains, legumes, herbs, oils, ferments, and spices; the generosity of seasons; and the endless ways flavor can be built, layered, and shared. This is plant-forward cooking grounded in my craft and guided by curiosity. Most importantly, it's a celebration of eating in a way that is joyful, nourishing, and deeply connected—to the land, to culture, and to one another. I invite you to cook boldly and discover the extraordinary magic of this bounty.

Where Cooking Begins

Plant-based cooking has reconnected me to my heritage. I am the daughter of Moroccan parents who immigrated to Spain from Fez in the early 1980s. I was born just off the Spanish coast outside Barcelona and grew up in Costa Brava—and now, nothing comforts me in the same way as an ocean breeze.

The culturally rich food traditions and spirituality of my Moroccan heritage were always present in our household—and cooking for each other has always been the answer to any kind of language barrier. I remember stories of my mother, the dutiful sister of seven young, orphaned children, resolving disagreements by bringing her siblings together around the dinner table and filling their bellies with comforting food. My family has shaped my respect for the act of breaking bread.

If you take a deeper look into traditional and indigenous food, many cultures already contain a vegan repertoire. In both Morocco and Spain, farm-to-table isn't a concept, it's a given. We eat what grows near us. Food waste is considered disrespectful to the people who grow it and the soil that once hosted those foods. I take that to heart. My grandmothers never ate at restaurants and, for them, cooking meals for their large families gave them power, pride, and strength. My family comes from North Africa, and its flavors are what I grew up with. Outside the walls of our home, the world was Spanish, and it became part of me too. These two cultures shaped my roots and gave me the foundation I needed to begin plant-based cooking.

Crossing Cultures

On top of my upbringing, my career has led me abroad, including to Bilbao, Spain; Modena, Italy; New York City, and Zurich, where I currently reside. (Never in my wildest dreams would I have imagined settling in Zurich, but I love living and working here in one of the most beautiful and diverse cities in Switzerland.) As you might expect, the food in these pages reflects a kaleidoscope of cultures.

The experiences I gathered traveling and cooking all over the world shaped the unique style we offer at my restaurants, and they have deeply influenced my home cooking as well. This is the result of my curiosity and my desire to blend cultures—especially those I have lived and worked within.

I used to love playing the board game Guess Who? in which you try to uncover your opponent's chosen character by asking identifying questions. When I started tasting the various foods of the world, I was reminded of this game, because there were so many similarities: the flatbread of one culture conjured up the flatbread of another; Russian *pelmeni* resembled tortellini; I could see the shared roots of *torrija* and French toast; and curry reminded me of mole. I discovered other parallels, some influenced by migrations or colonialism and some from indigenous cultures—arriving at similar outcomes with the ingredients available to them.

Since the anthropology of food is something I am passionate about, I wanted to share cross-cultural recipes without turning this book into a history lesson. We are all unique individuals, but I believe that to live in a kinder world, we should focus on what unites us: the cultural beliefs we share and the ways in which our identities are connected. This is why, over time, my cooking has become less about technique and more about intention.

The Hands Are Blessed

Cooking can be an expression of the emotional side of food: as generosity, familiarity, presence, and togetherness. In a world that rewards speed and constant output, this book aims to pull you back into the practice of cooking with purpose—cooking for yourself and cooking for connection. When you approach food with intention, the effect is larger than the action itself. It shapes how you care, how you choose, and how you relate to others. It supports your well-being in part because eating plants is simply good for the body.

When I started reducing animal products in my diet, I feared I might lose parts of who I am. Was I less Spanish if my tortilla didn't have eggs? Was I less Moroccan if my merguez didn't contain meat? Now I understand that none of that defines authenticity.

In Morocco, we say of many mothers' cooking, *yedd-ha mbaraka*—"her hands are blessed"—because care and intention give life to any dish. Cooking is a language, and there are endless ways to speak it. Avoiding animal products isn't a loss; it's a deliberate, meaningful choice that still leaves space for culture and expression.

How I Think About Food

Cooking at home feels very different from cooking in a restaurant, and I value both for different reasons. In my kitchens, everything moves fast and with intention, but at home there is greater space—to taste, to pause, to adjust. When I translate dishes from the restaurant to the home table, I'm not trying to re-create an experience or impress anyone. Flavor is still at the fore, but I slow down and prepare the food in a more personal way, and I cherish that freedom.

My approach to cooking is simple at its core: I start with what is in season, I pay attention to what ingredients naturally want to do, and I build flavor in layers until the dish feels alive. Over time, I've learned that great plant-based cooking isn't about chasing complexity—it's about making a few thoughtful choices, tasting with intention, and trusting my instincts. You can learn more about how to build flavors on page 15.

1. Ingredient quality — In the Mediterranean, vegetables are the heart of our nutrition, and the plants I use are the protagonists in my story. I encourage you to direct your own cast with the produce made available to you: cook what grows around you and source your ingredients responsibly.

2. Flavor relationships — I love making sense of the unexpected. I often start with an ingredient, then build contrast around it: something creamy or crunchy, bright and acidic against something rich, and perhaps something herbal or floral to lift the dish. By understanding a few reliable pairings, you'll have gained confidence in your choices.

3. *Sazón* — The Spanish expression *tener buen sazón* refers to having a skill for seasoning food; being described in this way is considered a greater honor than any college degree! Seasoning makes the difference.

Taste, smell, and touch everything in your kitchen. Listen to the different sounds of cooking. There is a nonverbal language in the crackles, sizzles, and pops. I understand seven verbal languages. But the language of cooking is my favorite. Reconnect with your intuition! Improvise! Take risks! Good cooking requires presence and mindfulness, both good things for you anyway.

How to Use This Book

Luckily for me, although cooking at home was not a priority for my parents, many other people populated our kitchen, keeping it alive. Both my grandmothers were known in the family for their culinary artistry, and all the aunts and cousins cooked grandiose feasts when they visited us, a Moroccan family living in the diaspora. And so, the romance of home cooking never disappeared. Thanks to them, I understood that cooking at home is a way to show love, not just to others but to yourself. It's a way to celebrate your identity, acknowledge those who came before you, and nourish those who come after.

Vegan Vegan! is a collection of dishes that bring me joy. These are dishes I love to either serve at the restaurant or make at home, prepared with produce and other ingredients readily available at most supermarkets. I hope it supports you in those moments you find yourself looking for inspiration and introduces you to new ingredients, techniques, and unexpected flavor combinations.

I want you to navigate the recipes with ease. Dietary and preparatory symbols (page 4) appear alongside each recipe, and you'll find tips throughout, offering small adjustments, shortcuts, or ways to push flavor a little further. Some dishes include variations to show how flexible they can be. I encourage you to treat these as suggestions instead of rules—use what you have, adapt to your preferences, and make the food your own. Once you feel comfortable with the cooking process, recipes can simply serve as starting points: it's then up to you whether you strictly adhere to them or adapt them with your own twists.

Cooking Toward the Future

In 2019, I received the keys to a space that would eventually house my first restaurant, Restaurant KLE. From the beginning, its purpose needed to be greater than myself—beyond ego or personal ambition—and be rooted instead in an impactful mission with a clear call to action through hospitality. Values such as sustainability, compassion, love, and empathy drove the final concept. Almost organically, it became evident that my challenge would be to feed the world without destroying the planet.

KLE had to be plant-based. I wanted to showcase the potential of cooking with a positive impact. There was just one complication: I truly enjoyed cheese and meat, and becoming vegan had never been part of my plan—until reality confronted me.

Intensive agriculture is rapidly deforesting the planet and destroying biodiversity. This homogenization of what we eat limits access to diverse, nourishing sources of nutrition. Less than 2 percent of the world's dairy production is organic, and the same is true for many other foods, including vegetables.

I try to make kinder choices for this beautiful planet and for the people and the animals that share it. I would be naive to believe that the whole world will become vegan, but we can still make a meaningful difference. Whether it's reducing meat consumption or getting to know the people who grow and harvest the food that nurtures you and your loved ones, every choice we make as consumers shapes the future of our environment. Plus, those choices ripple outward, influencing other areas of our lives, from fashion to cosmetics and beyond. We can all make a difference.

"Love" and "empathy" are powerful words, and I realized they needed to be reflected in the food we serve. Keeping an open mind, I began researching ways to cook with a lower carbon footprint and less environmental impact. Soon after opening my first restaurant, things began to take shape. Guests would ask for advice on how to incorporate more plant-based foods into their lives. Organic farmers became partners. The press started to put our work in the spotlight. The team grew stronger and more confident and, eventually, so did our food and my perspective. Unexpected Michelin stars and recognitions knocked at our door.

After my many years of traveling and working around the world, KLE reminded me of my values. The mission to change the industry and protect food is my North Star, and my restaurants are a manifestation of this. Everything, from the food on the plate to how we care for one another at the restaurants and beyond, is done with the purpose of inspiring with love. Cooking is an act of love, and by replacing some ingredients with plants, it can also become an act of revolution.

I believe cooking deserves a more central role in our lives. When we stop treating it as a tedious chore, it becomes a way to reconnect—with manual work, heritage, identity, and the language food carries. Cooking deserves time and space in our busy lives.

Caring Is Cool

I have witnessed firsthand how "caring" has led me to unimaginable places and has surrounded me with the most committed and kindest group of human beings. Organizing fundraiser events to support places experiencing food insecurity, speaking up for the basic universal human right to have access to food and clean water, and protecting and taking care of our farmers has become part of who we are at KLE.

Now, as the owner of three restaurants and a mentor to younger chefs, I have a different understanding of the industry, and I am committed to bringing change in every dimension possible and to always question how we can do better.

Sazón, Sazón! Building Flavor

Creating memorable flavor can feel daunting because it often involves trial and error. It's a test of how well you know your palate. I gravitate toward sour foods and love combining savory and sweet in mains. With practice, care, attentiveness, and a little patience, you can build confidence in your preferences. Once that's in place, you can push boundaries and expand your taste.

When tasting, connect deliberately with your palate and look for patterns. Taste is memory, and you can train it. With a strong base, you can keep layering to create more complex flavors. The first thing I do upon tasting a dish I'm working on is note how it makes me feel and what's present. Does it touch all the key taste notes? Is something out of balance? Does it need additional layers or dimensions?

When a dish is close but not completely there, some chefs feel compelled to rebuild it, but that puts all that hard work to waste. Instead, fine-tune it. Make one change at a time, taste often, and make adjustments only as needed. Small moves build reliable *sazón*... just like small habits build change.

Acidity	fruit vinegars, sumac, citrus, tamarind, sea buckthorn, fermented foods (kimchi, sauerkraut), unripe fruit (apple, papaya, mango), pineapple, berries, dairy-free sour cream, and yogurt
Aroma and depth	fresh and dried herbs and spices, harissa, chermoula
Bitterness	coffee, winter greens and collards (spring greens), dark chocolate, citrus rind, tahini
Nuttiness	fresh nuts and seeds (toast them or blend into nut butters or powders for finishing)
Saltiness	salts, soy sauce, preserved lemons, vegan garum, seaweed, pickles, foods preserved in salt or brine (olives, dried tomatoes), salt-fermented foods (kimchi, miso)
Sweetness	ripe and dried fruits, nuts, maple or fruit syrups, carrots, beans, sweet potatoes, pumpkin, jams, mirin; as a simple fix, cane or less-refined sugars
Umami	mushrooms, seaweeds, nutritional yeast, seed powders, almonds, umeboshi and fermented foods, soy sauce, balsamic reduction, olives, dried fruit and vegetables, capers, tomatoes, onions, garlic, nuts and legumes, plant-based yogurt and cream cheese, tomato paste (puree), tamari, black garlic, coconut aminos, gochujang, shio koji, hoisin, vegan ponzu

Trust Your Way

- Use memory as a tool; sharpen it. Nostalgia can point you toward knowledge.
- Keep a well-stocked pantry (with the ingredients listed above) so that you can fine-tune a dish quickly.
- Involve your senses—sight, taste, smell, touch, hearing—and, most importantly, your intuition.
- Learn the seasons and local growing cycles; syncing with nature clarifies choices.
- Observe how your ancestors and other cultures cook. Traditions live in us, and we can adapt them for the next generation and honor them as our own.
- Treat daily cooking as a creative canvas. Every meal is an opportunity for expression, to communicate feelings, memories, and ideas.

A Few Essential Ingredients

Some ingredients appear often in this book for good reason—they add depth, balance, or clarity with little effort. Think of them as helpful companions in the kitchen, ingredients that make plant-based cooking feel more confident, flexible, and generous.

Most can be found easily at well-stocked supermarkets, health-food stores, Asian and Middle Eastern grocers, or online. A few are worth making at home, where the process is part of the pleasure.

Apple honey (page 265)	This plant-based syrup is made by slowly reducing apple juice until concentrated and floral. I use it as an ingredient, adding sweetness in both savory and sweet dishes.
Aquafaba	This liquid from cooked chickpeas emulsifies, foams, and thickens —which is perfect for sauces, such as Benedict sauce (page 52) or meringues (page 225).
Espelette pepper	A mild chile from the Basque region. It has a gentle heat and a slightly sweet character. It adds warmth without overpowering a dish and works especially well as a finishing spice in recipes such as Scramble with Potatoes, Hot Honey, and Croutons (page 41).
Flaxseeds and chia seeds	When finely ground and hydrated, flaxseeds (linseeds) and chia seeds form a natural gel that binds batters and mixtures with gentle structure and moisture, much like egg would. Their neutral flavor supports both sweet and savory recipes.
Harissa paste	Made with dried chiles, garlic, spices, and oil, this North African chili paste can be smoky, fruity, or sharp. I love it as a flavored mayo (page 255).
Kala namak black salt	A mineral-rich salt with a sulfurous aroma that I use sparingly to add savory depth to scrambles and sauces. A little goes a long way.
Miso	A fermented soybean paste that adds salt, umami, and subtle sweetness. I use white or shiro miso as a seasoning instead of as a dominant flavor, often to flavor Hollandaise (page 55), emulsions (page 254), and spreads (page 88).
Nutritional yeast	A naturally savory ingredient with deep umami notes often used to create a "cheese" flavor.
Preserved lemon	Fresh lemons bring brightness but preserved lemons introduce depth. The fermented peel adds saltiness, bitterness, and complexity to dishes such as Bakoola (page 173).
Shokupan (page 68)	A soft Japanese milk bread, I use it for dishes that benefit from its tenderness and structure. It can also be substituted with any soft white loaf.
Smoked tofu	Smoked tofu is firm or extra-firm tofu infused with a smoky flavor, often from wood chips or tea leaves. Dense and savory, it adds depth and protein to dishes without needing to be pressed or cooked from raw.
Sweet smoky Spanish pimentón *(pimentón dulce)*	Sweet smoky Spanish pimentón is a spice made from red peppers that are slowly oak-smoked and finely ground, delivering deep warmth and gentle sweetness without heat to recipes such as the Paella Temaki (page 118). The most commonly used brand is La Chinata, prized for its intensity.

permanent marker
eva
ON TARE
OFF

Tools and Equipment

You don't need a professional kitchen to cook well, but a few reliable tools can make cooking smoother and more enjoyable. The items listed here are tools I use regularly, both at home and in my restaurants. They will help you to focus on what matters most: the ingredients and the flavor. With a few well-chosen essentials, cooking becomes more about enjoyment and less about managing the process.

Bench scraper and offset spatulas	Professional chefs always have plenty of these. They are perfect for cutting dough, transporting ingredients, and handling food in a skillet.
Cast-iron skillets	These are good long-term frying pans. Season them periodically with salt to cure the surface and prevent food from sticking to them.
Digital scale	A set of measuring cups and spoons are useful, but a digital scale will give you the most consistent results.
Fine-mesh strainer (sieve)	Passing sauces and stocks through a fine-mesh strainer (sieve) removes fibers and solids and gives purees and liquids a smoother and cleaner finish.
Food processor	A good food processor can handle tedious tasks at a fraction of the time it takes to do them with your hands.
Immersion blender	This allows you to process smaller amounts of food into creamy, smooth results—directly in the saucepan or pot.
Kitchen towels	Differentiate between wet towels for cleaning work surfaces and dry towels for handling hot baking sheets and pots. Reserve some clean towels solely for covering dough and touching food.
Knives	Paring (for peeling and fine detail work), santoku or chef's (for chopping, slicing, and everyday vegetable prep), and serrated knives (for bread, tomatoes, and ingredients with a tough exterior) are sharp! But they are also less dangerous than dull knives, because you don't need to apply pressure. Make sure you learn how to properly position your hands when cutting and chopping.
Painter's tape	Label all the food you cook with its name and the date it was prepared to help you keep your kitchen organized.
Ruler	Great for achieving consistent results when portioning.
Seasoning tray	This makes your seasoning process effortless. Place a tray next to your stove with basics like olive oil, table salt, kosher (coarse) salt, flaky salt, brown sugar, distilled white (malt) vinegar, red wine vinegar, nutritional yeast, Himalayan black salt, soy sauce, and chili paste.
Silicone baking mats	You can use these reusable silicone baking mats that line your baking sheets. This saves on parchment (baking) paper, and you avoid having to scrub crusty baking sheets for hours.
Timers	These little friends will help you stay organized.

II

RECIPES

Breakfast and Brunch

Breakfast and brunch often evoke a sense of comfort and familiar morning rituals. When I cook breakfast, soft textures, bright fruit, and warm breads offer a sense of calm and remind me why plant-based food has so much power. Even something as small as the scent of lavender in a muffin (page 26) or the steam rising from a just-made flatbread (page 76) can bring a quiet joy. Plants give us so many ways to build richness: the creaminess of silky hummus, the comfort of semolina, the brightness of fresh berries.

Of course, breakfast can also be playful. A batter can become airy pancakes (page 33), a plant-based scramble (page 40) will surprise you with its depth, even a crepe (page 30) can make it feel like a small celebration. Nothing here is complicated; I lean on flavors I trust. When these recipes come to life in your kitchen, enjoy them—and the pleasure of something warm and generous—as these bold dishes stand confidently on their own.

Blackberry-Lavender Muffins

My husband, Marc, is devoted to muffins. Whenever we stop for coffee, he orders one without fail, which frustrates me because I always hope he'll pick something we can share. Blackberry muffins are his favorite, so I set out to create a version I'd enjoy just as much.

The lavender adds a gentle floral note, the oats bring texture, and the flaky salt sharpens the contrast. I've always loved using flowers in sweets—orange blossom, violets, lavender—because they add delicacy and extend the flavor long after the bite. But the muffins also stand perfectly well on their own.

makes 6 large muffins

lavender syrup

½ cup (100 g) raw sugar
1 tablespoon dried organic lavender flowers
1 tablespoon lemon juice

batter

¾ cup (175 ml) unsweetened soy milk
zest of 1 lemon
2 tablespoons lemon juice
2 cups (240 g) all-purpose (plain) flour
¾ cup (180 g) raw sugar
2 teaspoons baking powder
½ teaspoon baking soda (bicarbonate of soda)
¼ teaspoon salt
¾ cup (170 g) soy yogurt
¼ cup (60 ml) sunflower oil
¼ cup (60 ml) extra-virgin olive oil
1 teaspoon vanilla extract
1 cup (130 g) blackberries, quartered
¼ cup (30 g) rolled (porridge) oats

to finish

¼ teaspoon flaky salt

method

lavender syrup

In a small pan, heat the sugar, lavender, and ½ cup (120 ml) water until almost boiling. Add the lemon juice, then remove from the heat. Let infuse for 30 minutes. Strain to remove the lavender and let cool.

batter

Preheat the oven to 350°F (180°C/ Gas Mark 4). Line a 6-cup muffin pan with muffin baking cups (cases).

Pour the milk into a bowl. Stir in the lemon zest and juice. Set aside to let curdle.

Sift the flour, sugar, baking powder, baking soda (bicarbonate of soda), and salt into a large bowl. Using a whisk, combine the curdled milk, yogurt, oils, and vanilla. Slowly whisk the milk mixture into the dry ingredients until just combined. To keep your muffins soft and fluffy, be careful not to overwork the batter; it should be runny but not too thin.

Spoon the batter into the muffin cups, placing a few blackberry pieces in the center of each muffin and the remainder overtop. Sprinkle over the oats. Bake for 25 minutes, or until a toothpick or skewer inserted into the center comes out clean. Remove from the oven.

to finish

While the muffins are still hot, drizzle with the lavender syrup and sprinkle with flaky salt. Transfer to a wire rack to cool.

Blueberry Flatbread with Cheese and Apple Honey

Typically sold by the slice in the streets of Morocco, *harsha* is a semolina flatbread with a coarse, textured exterior. (*Harsha* means "the rough one" in my Arabic dialect.) It can be stuffed with many different fillings. *Jben*, a traditional Moroccan cottage cheese, also sold by the slice in the streets, pairs perfectly with harsha. Together they make this delicious breakfast combo.

makes 4 flatbreads

jben

4 cups (about 1 liter) unsweetened soy milk
juice of 2 lemons
1 quantity Apple Honey (page 265)
pinch of salt

harsha

1½ cups (250 g) very coarse semolina, plus extra for coating
1 teaspoon baking powder
1 tablespoon raw sugar
¼ teaspoon salt
2 tablespoons sunflower oil, plus extra for shaping
⅔ cup (160 ml) unsweetened oat milk

to finish

⅔ cup (100 g) blueberries
¾ cup (100 g) shelled walnuts, toasted and crushed

method

jben

Bring the milk to a simmer in a saucepan over medium heat. Remove it from the heat, immediately add the lemon juice, and stir gently twice. Set it aside undisturbed for 30 minutes.

Line a sieve with cheesecloth (muslin) and set it over a bowl. Place the mixture in the sieve and refrigerate for at least 2 hours or overnight to drain. The cheese will become thick and creamy.

The next morning, season the jben with 1 tablespoon of the apple honey and the salt.

harsha

In a bowl, combine the semolina, baking powder, sugar, and salt. Add the sunflower oil and work it into the semolina with a clean hand until all the grains are coated. Gradually add the milk, mixing with your hand in a clawing motion until everything comes together. Cover the dough with a kitchen towel and let rest for 10 minutes. The dough should feel quite dry, almost like cookie dough.

Rub a little oil on your hands, shape the harsha into 4 equal balls, and coat them in coarse semolina. Gently flatten the harsha into discs, 1 inch (2.5 cm) thick.

Heat a nonstick skillet over low heat. Gently place the harsha in the pan and press a few blueberries into each one. Fry the harsha for 7 minutes on each side, until golden brown and cooked through.

assembly

Serve the harsha warm topped with a spoonful of the jben, the blueberries, a drizzle of apple honey and toasted walnuts.

Chef's Note: You can use a round cookie (biscuit) cutter to shape the discs into perfectly round harsha.

Crepes
with Chocolate-Hazelnut Spread and Whipped Cream

My dad worked a lot. He was always out of the house before we woke up and didn't return until late. Despite this, he created everlasting memories for my brother and me—we would spend time together in the kitchen whenever he had time off work. He used to bake my favorite strawberry cake, and on special occasions, he would make towering stacks of crepes that would last for days, so we could eat them for breakfast throughout the week before heading to school.

During berry or citrus seasons, I like to feature a crepe dessert at one of the restaurants as a tribute to those cherished memories, and here I share the recipe we use.

---

makes 6–8 crepes

chocolate-hazelnut spread

- 2 cups (250 g) shelled hazelnuts
- 1 cup (250 ml) unsweetened rice milk
- ⅓ cup (75 ml) maple syrup
- ¼ cup (60 ml) sunflower oil
- 1¾ ounces (50 g) vegan milk chocolate (44%), melted
- 3 tablespoons cacao powder (see Note)
- pinch of salt

crepe batter

- 2½ cups (600 ml) unsweetened soy milk
- 2 cups (240 g) all-purpose (plain) flour
- 3 tablespoons sunflower oil, plus extra for frying
- 2 tablespoons sugar
- ½ teaspoon vanilla extract or seeds of 1 vanilla bean

whipped cream

- 1 cup (250 ml) plant-based heavy (double) cream
- 1 tablespoon sugar
- 1 teaspoon vanilla powder

method

chocolate-hazelnut spread

Preheat the oven to 350°F (180°C/Gas Mark 4). Toast the hazelnuts for 5 minutes, until golden brown. Let cool a little, then process them in a blender to a smooth nut butter. Add the remaining ingredients and blend until smooth.

crepe batter

In a bowl, blend all the ingredients with an immersion blender until smooth. The batter should be loose enough to spread thinly and easily in a pan. Let rest for 15 minutes.

whipped cream

Whip all the ingredients in a bowl with a hand mixer until it holds its shape.

assembly

Heat an 11-inch (28-cm) nonstick skillet over medium heat. Brush with a little oil. Spoon a ladleful of the crepe batter into the pan and swirl it around until the bottom of the pan is coated with a thin layer. Pour any excess batter back into the bowl.

Cook the crepe until set. Flip it and cook on the other side until browned. Repeat with the rest of the batter.

Serve the crepes filled and drizzled with the chocolate-hazelnut spread and a spoonful of whipped cream.

Chef's Note: Cacao powder comes from unroasted or lightly processed cacao beans, which means it keeps more of the bean's natural sharpness, bitterness, and chocolate aroma. It tastes brighter and more intense than cocoa powder.

Fluffy Pancakes with Three Chocolates

These pancakes are the American-style version we served for brunch at KLE when we first opened. Guests still talk about these pancakes.

makes 6 pancakes

batter

2⅓ cups (290 g) all-purpose (plain) flour
⅓ cup (65 g) raw sugar
2 tablespoons baking powder
½ teaspoon salt
2 teaspoons apple cider vinegar
seeds of 1 vanilla bean
1½ cups (350 ml) unsweetened oat milk
sunflower oil, for frying

toppings

10½ ounces (300 g) vegan dark chocolate
7 ounces (200 g) vegan white chocolate
7 ounces (200 g) vegan milk chocolate
1¾ cups (200 g) toasted slivered (flaked) almonds (optional)

method

batter

Preheat the oven to 350°F (180°C/Gas Mark 4).

In a stand mixer, whisk together the pancake batter ingredients. Only whisk as long as needed for the ingredients to come together in a smooth batter. Let rest for 15 minutes while you prepare your toppings.

toppings

Melt the three chocolates separately over a double boiler or bain marie or in the microwave. Toast the almonds in the oven for 5 minutes, or until golden brown.

assembly

Heat a 6-inch (15-cm) skillet over medium heat and brush it with a little sunflower oil. Pour a generous amount of batter into the pan to create a ½-inch (1-cm) tall pancake. Reduce the heat to low and cook for 5 minutes, until the edges are set and golden brown. Flip the pancake and cook until golden brown underneath. For extra soft and fluffy pancakes, cover the pan with a lid while cooking to keep the moisture in.

Transfer the pancakes to plates. Spread the dark chocolate overtop, and drizzle over the other two melted chocolates. Top with the slivered almonds, if desired.

Chef's Note: To create a beautiful decoration, drizzle the white and milk chocolates in a spiral pattern, then run the tip of a knife from the center to the edges of the pancakes.

Savory Baghrir with Merguez Crumble and Harissa Mayo

Baghrir are yeast pancakes traditional in Morocco, Algeria, and Tunisia. When made well, they are heavenly fluffy and feel like a cloud in your mouth. Although they look similar to Ethiopian *injera*, their taste is different.

You'll find both sweet and savory serving suggestions here, but my personal favorite is simply drizzling them with olive oil and apple honey. Photo on page 36.

---

makes 8–10 pancakes

pancakes

1½ cups (260 g) fine semolina
1½ cups (260 g) coarse semolina
1 tablespoon baking powder
2 teaspoons active dry yeast
1 teaspoon salt

merguez crumble

1 cup (200 g) dried cranberry (borlotti) or fava (broad) beans, soaked in water overnight (or 2¾ cups/400 g cooked beans)
1 cup (180 g) red rice
3 cloves garlic, minced
1 onion, diced
1 bunch cilantro (coriander), coarsely chopped
1 bunch parsley, coarsely chopped
½ cup (30 g) nutritional yeast
⅓ cup (100 g) harissa paste (puree)
¼ cup (70 g) tomato paste
¼ cup (60 ml) extra-virgin olive oil
2 tablespoons smoked paprika
1½ tablespoons ground cumin
1½ tablespoons ground coriander
1 teaspoon salt

Moroccan salad

1 baby gem lettuce heart, sliced
1 tomato, finely chopped
1 red onion, finely chopped
½ cucumber, finely chopped
1 small bunch mint, finely chopped
1 small bunch parsley, finely chopped
1 small bunch cilantro (coriander), finely chopped
pinch of salt
pinch of black pepper
extra-virgin olive oil
juice of ½ lemon

assembly

Harissa Mayo (page 254), for drizzling

method

pancakes

Put all the ingredients into a bowl. Slowly whisk in 3¾ cups (900 ml) of lukewarm water. Use an immersion blender to mix the batter until smooth. Let rest for 15–20 minutes.

Heat a nonstick skillet over medium-high heat. Blend the batter again with an immersion blender to incorporate some air and create bubbles on the surface. Spoon a ladleful of batter into the pan to form a thin pancake. Small holes will begin to appear on top, creating a honeycomb pattern. These pancakes are cooked on one side only.

Transfer the pancake to a plate and cover it with a clean kitchen towel. Repeat the process with the remaining batter. If bubbles don't appear on the surface, the batter needs to rest longer—be patient, because it takes time and practice to know the perfect moment to cook the pancakes.

You can reheat the pancakes in a steam oven or by steaming them in a colander over a pan of boiling water.

merguez crumble

Drain the soaked beans, then cook in boiling water for 45 minutes, or until softened. (Skip this step if using cooked beans.)

In a separate pan, cook the red rice according to the package directions. Drain the beans and rice and let cool for a few minutes. Blend with the remaining merguez crumble ingredients in a food processor until it forms a chunky paste.

In a nonstick skillet over medium heat, fry the merguez until crumbly like ground (minced) meat.

Moroccan salad

Combine the lettuce, tomato, onion, cucumber, and herbs in a bowl. Season with the salt, pepper, olive oil, and lemon juice just before serving.

assembly

Place the pancakes on a plate and top with the merguez crumble, salad, and a drizzle of the harissa mayo. Roll up like a wrap and serve.

Sweet Baghrir with Orange Blossom Custard and Orange Syrup

These pancakes sit somewhere between breakfast and dessert, bringing together soft, warm stacks with a fragrant orange blossom custard and a bright citrus syrup.

The orange syrup provides a clean, vibrant contrast, lifted with a touch of olive oil for a rounded finish. Spoon everything generously over the pancakes and finish with toasted pistachios for crunch. It's light yet layered and balances sweetness, acidity and texture in an elegant way. Photo on page 37.

makes 8–10 pancakes

orange blossom custard

2 tablespoons cornstarch (cornflour)
2 cups (475 ml) plant-based light (single) cream
¼ cup (50 g) raw sugar
seeds of 1 vanilla bean
pinch of ground turmeric
½ teaspoon orange blossom water

orange syrup

zest of 1 orange
juice of 2 oranges
½ cup (100 g) raw sugar
1 tablespoon extra-virgin olive oil

to finish

1 quantity pancakes (page 34), warmed
shelled pistachios, toasted and chopped
seasonal fruit (optional)

method

orange blossom custard

Stir the cornstarch (cornflour) with ¼ cup (60 ml) water until smooth. Bring the cream, sugar, vanilla seeds, and turmeric to a boil in a saucepan. Whisk in the cornstarch slurry and cook for 2 minutes over medium heat, whisking continuously until the custard has thickened.

Remove the custard from the heat and stir in the orange blossom water. Cover the surface with plastic wrap (clingfilm) to prevent a skin from forming and set aside to cool.

orange syrup

In a small pan, heat the orange zest, juice, sugar, and ⅓ cup (75 ml) water, stirring until the sugar has dissolved. Stir in the olive oil. Remove from the heat and pour into a small pitcher (jug).

to finish

Place 2–3 pancakes on each plate. Pour over a generous amount of the orange syrup. Drizzle with the custard and sprinkle with the chopped pistachios. Finish with seasonal fruit if desired.

Custard Tarts with Spinach and Feta-Style Cheese

Sometimes you want to get ahead and organize items for your next brunch or breakfast in advance. These little tarts or pies are something you can prebake and reheat before serving.

The smoked tofu brings a nice depth and umami flavor to the tarts, balanced by the acidity and tanginess from the cheese.

---

makes 6 tarts

sunflower or vegetable oil, for frying and greasing
1 large leek, white and light green parts only, thinly sliced
1 clove garlic, minced
¼ teaspoon salt
3 large handfuls spinach (about 5 oz/150 g)
¼ nutmeg, grated
black pepper
juice of ½ lemon
3½ ounces (100 g) smoked tofu, coarsely grated
1 quantity "Egg" Custard batter (page 55)
½ cup (75 g) Feta-Style Cheese (page 263), chilled for 3 hours
1 (11-oz/320-g) package vegan puff pastry
all-purpose (plain) flour, for dusting

method

Heat a drizzle of oil in a skillet over medium heat. Add the leek, garlic, and salt, and sauté for 5 minutes, until the leeks are softened. Stir in the spinach and cook until wilted. Season with the grated nutmeg, pepper, and lemon juice. Set aside.

Heat a drizzle of oil in a skillet over high heat. Add the smoked tofu and cook for 10 minutes, until brown and caramelized. Stir the fried tofu into the "egg" custard batter.

Preheat the oven to 350°F (180°C/Gas Mark 4).

Roll out the puff pastry on a lightly floured surface and cut it into 6 circles, each 4 inches (10 cm) in diameter.

Lightly grease a muffin pan with a little oil. Place the pastry circles in the pan, pressing gently into the corners. Brush each pastry cup with oil, then fill them with the egg custard and top with a spoonful of sautéed spinach.

Bake the tarts in the oven for 20 minutes. Crumble the "cheese" on top and return to the oven for a final 5 minutes, or until the pastry is golden brown and the custard has set.

Scramble with Caramelized Onions and Chebakia Spices

A scramble is such a simple dish, yet incredibly satisfying. I honestly doubted that anything plant-based could truly hit the mark for a scramble, but this recipe does. The chebakia spices—a Moroccan blend typically used for the sesame pastry chebakia, combining warm spices like cinnamon and anise—add a subtle sweetness and depth. I like to keep it simple with a garnish of chives, and served with Shokupan (page 68), but feel free to create your own combos—serve it with roasted nuts, labneh, hummus, taktouka, salsa, XO sauce, seed mixes, chili oil—there are so many creative options! Photo on page 43.

serves 4

basic scramble

- 1 pound (500 g) medium-firm tofu
- 9 ounces (250 g) silken tofu
- ½ cup (120 ml) plant-based light (single) cream
- 1 tablespoon nutritional yeast
- ½ teaspoon ground turmeric
- ½ teaspoon kala namak black salt, plus extra to taste
- ½ teaspoon salt, plus extra to taste
- ½ teaspoon black pepper
- margarine, for frying

caramelized onion

- 4 onions, thinly sliced
- sunflower oil, for frying
- pinch of salt
- 2 teaspoons ground anise seeds
- 2 teaspoons ground cinnamon
- 1 teaspoon ground turmeric
- 1 quantity Hummus (page 83)
- extra-virgin olive oil, for drizzling
- toasted flaked almonds, for sprinkling

method

basic scramble

In a large bowl, crumble the tofu with your hands. Using gloves (to prevent staining), hand-mix in the remaining ingredients.

Heat the margarine in a skillet over medium-high heat. Add the scramble and pan-fry for 5–10 minutes. Add a little more cream if you prefer a runny consistency. Season to taste with more black salt or salt.

caramelized onion

Place the onions in a skillet with a drizzle of sunflower oil and salt. Cook them slowly over medium-low heat for 1 hour, stirring often, until caramelized.

Mix the spices together in a small bowl. Place a generous spoonful of the hummus in a shallow dish. Using the tip of the spoon, press down into the center and, in one smooth motion, rotate the spoon while spinning the plate in the opposite direction to create a circular shape with raised edges.

assembly

Spoon the warm scramble into the center of the hummus ring. Top with the caramelized onions. Drizzle generously with olive oil and sprinkle with the spices. Finish with the toasted flaked almonds.

Scramble with Potatoes, Hot Honey, and Croutons

This dish leans into contrast: softly set vegan scramble against crisp potatoes, crunchy croutons, and a glossy drizzle of sweet heat. The hot honey—maple syrup sharpened with Sriracha and lemon—catches on the croutons and pools lightly over the scramble. Black salt deepens the eggy flavor, while Espelette adds gentle warmth. A generous, layered dish designed for sharing, with texture in every bite. Photo on page 42.

serves 4

basic scramble
- 1 pound (500 g) medium-firm tofu
- 9 ounces (250 g) silken tofu
- ½ cup (120 ml) plant-based light (single) cream
- 1 tablespoon nutritional yeast
- ½ teaspoon ground turmeric
- ½ teaspoon kala namak black salt, plus extra to taste
- ½ teaspoon salt, plus extra to taste
- ½ teaspoon black pepper
- margarine, for frying

croutons
- 7 ounces (200 g) stale bread, cut into large cubes
- 1 clove garlic, minced
- ¼ cup (60 ml) extra-virgin olive oil
- 1 tablespoon chopped parsley
- ¼ teaspoon salt
- ¼ teaspoon black pepper
- zest of 1 lemon

hot honey
- ⅓ cup (75 ml) maple syrup
- 2 tablespoons Sriracha
- 1 tablespoon extra-virgin olive oil
- 1 teaspoon lemon juice

potatoes
- 4 large potatoes, peeled and cut into 1-inch (2-cm) cubes
- 1 teaspoon salt
- sunflower oil, for frying
- pinch of kala namak black salt
- pinch of Espelette pepper
- 1 handful parsley, chopped

method

basic scramble
In a large bowl, crumble the tofu with your hands. Using gloves (to prevent staining), hand-mix in the remaining ingredients.

Heat the margarine in a skillet over medium-high heat. Add the scramble and pan-fry for 5–10 minutes. Add a little more cream if you prefer a runny consistency. Season to taste with more black salt or salt.

croutons
Preheat the oven to 350°F (180°C/ Gas Mark 4).

Combine all the ingredients in a bowl. Transfer to a baking sheet. Bake for 5–10 minutes, until golden and crunchy.

hot honey
Whisk together the ingredients in a bowl.

potatoes
Put the potatoes in a saucepan and cover with water. Add the salt to the water and bring to a boil. Cook the potatoes for 20–30 minutes, until a paring knife easily slides through the center. Drain the potatoes, then let steam dry for a few minutes.

Heat a drizzle of oil in a skillet over high heat. Add the potatoes and pan-fry until golden and crunchy on the outside. Add the salt and Espelette pepper, then remove from the heat.

assembly
Serve the warm scramble topped with the potatoes in a serving dish. In a bowl, toss the croutons with the hot honey to nicely glaze, and scatter them over the scramble. Finish with a drizzle of the hot honey, a pinch each of black salt and Espelette pepper and chopped parsley.

Crème Brûlée French Toast

This recipe celebrates the way a simple idea travels across cultures. What began as *pain perdu*—a classic way to revive day-old bread—has taken many forms, from French toast to Spanish *torrija*. Soft shokupan bread gives it a tender crumb, while warm spice and citrus keep the flavors balanced. It's familiar, but with just enough variation to make it feel new. Photo on page 46.

---

makes 4 slices

crème brûlée
- 2¼ cups (500 ml) plant-based light (single) cream
- 1½ tablespoons cornstarch (cornflour)
- ½ cup (100 g) raw sugar
- 1 cinnamon stick
- 1 teaspoon vanilla powder or seeds of 1 vanilla bean
- pinch of ground turmeric
- pinch of kala namak black salt
- 1 strip of orange peel
- 1 strip of lemon peel

French toast
- 2 cups (475 ml) unsweetened oat milk
- ¼ cup (50 g) raw sugar
- 1 teaspoon ground cinnamon
- 1 teaspoon vanilla powder
- pinch of salt
- 1 tablespoon chia or flaxseeds, finely blended
- 1 tablespoon all-purpose (plain) flour
- 4 thick slices Shokupan (page 68)
- scant ½ cup (100 g) margarine

assembly
- ¼ cup (60 g) sugar

method

crème brûlée

In a small bowl, whisk together 2 tablespoons of the cream with the cornstarch (cornflour) until smooth.

Heat the remaining cream in a saucepan with the sugar, cinnamon, vanilla, turmeric, black salt, and citrus peels. When hot, add the cornstarch slurry and bring to a boil. Cook for 2–3 minutes, whisking continuously until the custard has thickened.

Pour the custard into a container and cover the surface with plastic wrap (clingfilm) to prevent a skin from forming. Let cool in the refrigerator for 2 hours, or until set.

Once set, remove the cinnamon stick and citrus peels. Blend the custard in a food processor or with an immersion blender until smooth.

French toast

In a saucepan, heat the milk, sugar, cinnamon, vanilla powder, and salt until the sugar has dissolved. Whisk in the chia (or flaxseed) powder and flour.

Pour the milk mixture into a shallow dish. Add the bread and soak them for at least 20 minutes, turning them over after 10 minutes.

Melt the margarine in a large nonstick skillet over medium heat. Add the bread and fry for 4 minutes on each side until a beautiful golden-brown crust has formed.

assembly

Spread a spoonful of the custard on each slice of French toast. Sprinkle with sugar, then use a kitchen blowtorch to create a caramelized crust. If you don't have one, you can use the broiler of your oven or the back of a heated metal spoon.

French Toast with Brigadeiro

30'

Golden, custardy slices of French toast meet the rich, fudgy sweetness of *brigadeiro*, Brazil's beloved chocolate confection made with condensed milk and cocoa. As it melts into the warm bread, the brigadeiro creates a glossy, indulgent coating that turns a familiar breakfast into something more dessert-like. Photo on page 47.

---

makes 4 slices

brigadeiro
2 cups (475 ml) unsweetened rice milk
1 cup (250 ml) plant-based light (single) cream
1¼ cups (250 g) sugar
2 ounces (55 g) vegan dark chocolate
1 tablespoon cacao powder
pinch of salt

assembly
1 quantity French Toast (page 44)
⅔ cup (100 g) sesame seeds, toasted
⅔ cup (100 g) peanuts, toasted and chopped

method

brigadeiro
Combine the ingredients in a saucepan, and cook over low heat, stirring often until reduced by half.

Add the dark chocolate to the warm condensed milk and stir until the chocolate has melted. Whisk in the cacao powder and salt.

assembly
Spread a generous spoonful of the brigadeiro over the French toast. Top with the toasted sesame seeds and peanuts.

Tortilla de Patatas

When I worked in Bilbao and needed a hearty breakfast to power through a long, exhausting day, *tortilla de patatas* was always my go-to. This delicious and satisfying potato omelet is a staple in Spanish households, appearing regularly for breakfast, lunch, or dinner.

This version, which we serve at our wine bar, COR, is one of my favorites. I love it served on top of *pan con tomate*, just like a classic *pintxo*.

---

serves 4

tortilla

- 2¼ pounds (1 kg) onions, finely sliced
- 4 cups (1 liter) vegetable oil, plus extra for frying
- generous pinch of salt
- 1 pound (500 g) potatoes, sliced into ¼-inch (5-mm) thick rounds

batter

- ½ cup (45 g) chickpea (gram) flour
- 14 ounces (400 g) silken tofu
- 1 cup + 2 tablespoons (275 ml) unsweetened soy milk
- ⅓ cup (65 g) potato starch
- 1 teaspoon baking powder
- 1 teaspoon salt
- ½ teaspoon black pepper
- ¼ teaspoon kala namak black salt
- pinch of ground turmeric

assembly

- vegetable oil, for frying
- Vegan Aioli (page 254) or your favorite mayonnaise (pages 254–255)

method

tortilla

Put the onions into a pan over medium-low heat, drizzle over some vegetable oil, and sprinkle with the salt. Cook for 1 hour, stirring often, until softened and caramelized.

Meanwhile, put the potatoes into a separate saucepan and cover with the vegetable oil. Cook over medium-low heat for 30 minutes, stirring occasionally to prevent them from sticking to the bottom of the pan, until a paring knife easily slides through the center. Let cool in the oil, then drain.

batter

Preheat the oven to 325°F (160°C/Gas Mark 3).

Spread the chickpea (gram) flour on a baking sheet. Bake for 30 minutes, stirring every 10 minutes. Remove the flour and increase the oven temperature to 350°F (180°C/ Gas Mark 4). Let the flour cool, then blend with the remaining ingredients until completely smooth.

assembly

In a large bowl, mix together the caramelized onions, confit potatoes, and batter.

Heat 1 tablespoon of oil in a nonstick ovenproof skillet over medium heat. Pour the mixture into the pan and reduce the heat to low. Using a spatula, evenly distribute the onions and potatoes. Cover with a lid and cook for 10 minutes, or until the edges have started to set.

Remove the lid and place the pan in the oven for 10 minutes, or until the tortilla top has set. Remove from the oven and place a plate on top. Flip the tortilla out onto the plate, then slide it carefully back into the pan. Cook over low heat for 10 minutes, or until golden brown underneath. Flip the tortilla onto a plate and let cool a little before slicing. Serve with a spoonful of aioli (or your favorite mayonnaise).

Apricot Tamales with Kimchi

This is one of the oldest dishes on the tasting menu at KLE. We wanted to bring together the influence that Mexican, French, Swiss, and Korean cuisines had on our culinary training. I think a bite of this dish perfectly encapsulates it all. The uniqueness of nixtamalized corn, the whipped cream, the glossy apricot jam, and the punchy kimchi make this tamale an unforgettable bite.

---

serves 6

pickled carrots
- 2 carrots, shaved into ribbons
- ½ cup (120 ml) tarragon vinegar
- ½ cup (120 ml) white vinegar
- 3 tablespoons sugar
- 4 teaspoons salt

apricot jam
- 2¼ pounds (1 kg) ripe apricots, quartered
- ¾ cup (150 g) sugar
- ⅔ cup (150 ml) white wine
- 3½ tablespoons margarine

tamales
- 1 cup + 2 tablespoons (250 g) margarine
- 1 pound (500 g) masa harina (nixtamalized corn flour)
- 2 banana leaves
- ⅓ cup (100 g) apricot jam (see above)
- ¼ cup (50 g) kimchi, finely chopped
- 2½ teaspoons salt
- 2 teaspoons baking powder
- pinch of black pepper

carrot jus
- 8½ cups (2 liters) carrot juice
- 1 tablespoon cornstarch (cornflour)
- ½ cup (120 ml) extra-virgin olive oil
- 1 teaspoon salt

carrot cream
- 2 tablespoons extra-virgin olive oil
- 2 shallots, thinly sliced
- ½ teaspoon salt
- 3 carrots, finely diced
- 2 cardamom pods
- 1 teaspoon tarragon vinegar
- 1 cup (250 ml) vegetable stock

to serve
- 3 banana leaves
- 1 handful carrot leaves

method

pickled carrots
The day before, pickle the carrots to allow time for the flavors to develop. Heat 2 cups (475 ml) water, the vinegars, sugar, and salt in a saucepan until the salt and sugar have dissolved. Place the carrot ribbons in a jar and pour the hot pickling liquid over them. Seal the jar and cool to room temperature. Store in the refrigerator overnight.

apricot jam
You can either use store-bought preserves or make this jam. To make your own, place the apricot quarters in a large saucepan with the sugar and white wine. Cook over medium-high heat, stirring often, for 15–20 minutes, until most of the liquid has evaporated. Stir in the margarine and remove from the heat. Let cool.

tamales
Beat the margarine in a stand mixer fitted with the beater attachment on high speed for 10 minutes, until pale and fluffy. Add the masa and beat for another 2 minutes. Add the remaining ingredients and ¼ cup (60 ml) water, and beat for 10 minutes, or until well emulsified and fluffy.

Cut the banana leaves into six 11-inch (28-cm) strips. Use scissors to cut away the tough stem. Soften the leaves by toasting them lightly in a pan.

Lay out the banana leaves on a clean work surface. Divide the masa mixture between them, placing it in the middle of each leaf.

To wrap the tamales, fold one long side of the banana leaf over the masa mixture. Fold the other long side over the top to envelop it completely. Flip the tamale over, then fold both open ends of the banana leaf underneath, gently pressing to shape the tamale into a neat rectangle. Steam the tamales for 1 hour, or until set like a very moist sponge cake.

carrot jus
Simmer the carrot juice in a saucepan over medium heat until reduced by half. In a small bowl, mix the cornstarch (cornflour) with 1 tablespoon water until smooth. Add the cornstarch slurry to the carrot juice along with the olive oil and salt. Bring to a boil while whisking, then cook the jus (still whisking) for 2–3 minutes, until slightly thickened.

carrot cream
Heat the oil in a saucepan over medium heat. Add the shallots and salt and sauté for 5 minutes, or until softened. Add the carrots and cardamom and cook until the carrots are caramelized.

Deglaze the pan with the vinegar. Pour in the stock and cook for 5–7 minutes, until the carrots are softened. Remove from the heat and let the mixture cool a little. Discard the cardamom pods. Blend with an immersion blender until smooth.

assembly
Cut each banana leaf into 2 squares. Line each of six individual serving plates with a square. Once the tamales are cooked, carefully unwrap them and place one on each of the prepared plates. Top the tamales with a spoonful each of the carrot cream and apricot jam. Garnish with pickled carrot ribbons and carrot leaves. Serve with the warm carrot jus on the side, to be poured at the table.

M’hammarin Potatoes Benedict

While I was living in New York City, I’d eat Benedict over brioche bread on the weekends. I tend to cling to food memories until I make something out of them. When I was considering a change to the brunch menu at DAR, this idea of Benedict potatoes sprung to mind, and I was pleasantly surprised by the results.

M’hammarin in Arabic means to turn something into a reddish color—in this case, potatoes tossed in harissa sauce.

serves 4

Benedict sauce

½ cup (120 ml) aquafaba
1 teaspoon Dijon mustard
pinch of salt
pinch of kala namak black salt
1 tablespoon lemon juice
1 cup (200 g) margarine, melted and warm

potatoes

1 pound (500 g) small new potatoes
1 tablespoon salt
1 tablespoon extra-virgin olive oil
3 tablespoons harissa paste
1 bunch chives, finely chopped

method

Benedict sauce
Combine all the ingredients except the margarine in a bowl. Using an immersion blender, blend until smooth. Slowly add the margarine, blending continuously to emulsify the mixture. Set aside.

potatoes
Bring a saucepan of water to a boil. Add the potatoes and salt and cook for 30 minutes, or until the potatoes can be easily pierced with a knife. Drain, then let cool a little.

Cut the potatoes in half, or into quarters if they are large.

Heat the olive oil in a skillet over medium-high heat. Add the potatoes and fry for 10 minutes, or until golden brown. Stir in the harissa and cook for another 2 minutes.

Transfer the potatoes to a large serving bowl. Top with the Benedict sauce and chopped chives.

Hollandaise Omelet

An eggless omelet might sound absurd to some people, but with this one, with its delicate, thin "skin" encasing an airy Hollandaise-style foam, it's hard to believe that no eggs were used in the process. This isn't the easiest of recipes, because it requires technique and you may need to practice a few times to master the perfect thickness. But trust me, it's worth it.

serves 4

Hollandaise

½ cup (120 ml) aquafaba
2 tablespoons shiro miso paste
1 tablespoon capers
1 tablespoon tarragon vinegar
1 teaspoon Dijon mustard
1 teaspoon nutritional yeast
1 teaspoon onion powder
1 teaspoon garlic powder
pinch of smoked paprika
pinch of kala namak black salt
1 cup (250 ml) sunflower oil

"egg" custard

4½ ounces (125 g) silken tofu
¼ cup (30 g) cornstarch (cornflour)
1 teaspoon nutritional yeast
½ teaspoon baking powder
¼ teaspoon kala namak black salt
¼ teaspoon salt
pinch of ground turmeric
¼ cup (60 ml) vegetable stock
1 teaspoon soy sauce
1 teaspoon mirin
margarine or sunflower oil, for frying
mixed green salad or pickles, to serve (optional)

method

Hollandaise

Combine all the ingredients except the oil in a tall pitcher (jug). Blend using an immersion blender. With the blender running, slowly drizzle in the sunflower oil to emulsify. Blend until smooth with the consistency of heavy (double) cream.

Strain the sauce through a fine-mesh strainer (sieve), then pour into a siphon bottle. Charge the siphon with a cream charger, shake well, and test the foam on a small plate. It should hold its shape; if not, add a second charge. Refrigerate until ready to serve.

"egg" custard

Put the dry ingredients, followed by the wet, into a bowl. Blend until completely smooth.

Heat a nonstick skillet over medium heat and brush it with a little melted margarine or sunflower oil. Spoon a ladleful of the omelet batter into the pan and gently swirl it so that the batter covers the bottom of the pan in a thin layer. Fry for 2–3 minutes, until completely cooked and dry but not crispy. Gently slide the omelet onto a plate and cover half with the Hollandaise foam. Fold the omelet over to cover the foam, creating an envelope.

Serve immediately, with a simple mixed green salad or pickles, if you like.

Sunchoke Hash Brown

Potato patties are beloved snacks for many. In Morocco, we call them *maakouda*, in Indonesia they're known as *perkedel kentang*, and in other places as hash browns. Cooks have been grating potatoes into a pan for the longest time, and there are hundreds of variations. The recipe we created doesn't have potatoes in it—we used sunchokes instead. The sunchoke is less starchy but it makes the patties juicier than potatoes would.

serves 4

6 sunchokes
3 tablespoons extra-virgin olive oil
1 onion, finely chopped
2 cloves garlic, crushed
2 tablespoons chickpea (gram) flour
1 tablespoon cilantro (coriander), finely chopped
1 teaspoon ground turmeric
pinch of salt
pinch of black pepper
Labneh (page 262) or Preserved Lemon–Mustard Mayo (page 255), to serve

method

Steam the sunchokes for 1–1½ hours, until a knife slides through them easily. Peel and pulse in a food processor until you have a chunky mash. Place the sunchoke mash in cheesecloth (muslin) and squeeze out as much of the liquid as possible.

Heat 2 tablespoons of oil in a skillet over medium heat. Add the onions and garlic and sauté for 7 minutes, or until soft but not colored.

Add the onion mixture to the sunchoke mash. Mix together with the remaining ingredients. With oiled hands, shape the mixture into 4 patties.

Heat a tablespoon of oil in a skillet over medium heat. Add the hash browns and fry for 10 minutes on each side, until golden brown and crunchy. Transfer to paper towels to drain any excess oil. Serve with labneh or preserved lemon-mustard mayo.

Smoked Peas and Blueberries with Vanilla Hollandaise

This may be the most refined and complex dish in this chapter—not in technique but in concept. This is a recipe showcasing how peas, smoke, and vanilla are the perfect match. The smoke aroma brings savoriness to the sweet peas, while the vanilla Hollandaise adds a sophisticated touch.

serves 4

vanilla Hollandaise
juice of ¼ lemon
½ cup (120 ml) aquafaba
2 tablespoons shiro miso paste
1 tablespoon maple syrup
¼ teaspoon vanilla extract
pinch of ground turmeric
pinch of kala namak black salt
pinch of salt
1 cup (250 ml) sunflower oil

smoked peas
1 pound (500 g) peas in pods, shelled
seed oil (optional)
1¾ cups (250 g) blueberries
olive oil, for drizzling
pinch of flaky salt
seeds of ½ vanilla bean

assembly
1 handful pea shoots (optional)

method

vanilla Hollandaise
Preheat a charcoal grill.

Using an immersion blender, combine all the ingredients except the oil in a pitcher (jug). Slowly drizzle in the sunflower oil, blending continuously to emulsify until the mixture is thick and smooth.

Fill a siphon bottle with the sauce and charge it once. Shake well and test on a small plate. The foam should hold its shape. If it doesn't, add another charge to the bottle. Refrigerate until needed.

smoked peas
Put the peas in a metal sieve and place on the grill. Cook gently for 3–4 minutes, making sure the smoke engulfs the peas to infuse them with smokiness, until some peas have charred. A little seed oil on the peas can help speed up this process.

Combine the peas and blueberries in a bowl. Add a drizzle of olive oil, the flaky salt, and seeds of the vanilla bean.

assembly
Scoop the peas on one side of the bowl and the Hollandaise into the other side. Garnish with pea shoots when available.

Doughnut Bikini

As this dish demonstrates, I am strongly influenced by American culture, including *The Simpsons*. As a child, American doughnuts weren't part of my reality, so I idolized them. A "bikini" is what we call a ham and cheese sandwich in Barcelona.

Here, I reimagine that sandwich with a savory, deli-style filling tucked inside a doughnut and cooked like a grilled sandwich. Don't judge me before tasting it!

---

serves 4

- ½ cup (125 g) high-gluten (very strong) flour
- ⅓ cup (70 g) cooked cannellini beans
- ¼ cup (15 g) nutritional yeast
- 1½ teaspoons smoked paprika
- 1½ teaspoons onion powder
- 1½ teaspoons garlic powder
- ½ teaspoon dried thyme
- ½ teaspoon dried parsley
- ½ teaspoon dried oregano
- ¼ teaspoon salt
- ½ cup (120 ml) vegetable (stock)
- 1 tablespoon apple cider vinegar

to serve

- 4 plain or maple-glazed vegan doughnuts
- 1 cup (350 g) Labneh (page 262), vegan cream cheese, or Cashew-Miso Spread (page 88)
- 3½ tablespoons margarine, for frying
- confectioners' (icing) sugar, for dusting

method

Place all the ingredients in a bowl. Using gloves, mix with your hands, pressing to break the beans and incorporate all the seasoning ingredients. Season with salt.

Gently shape the mixture into a uniform cylinder by tightly wrapping it in a sheet of plastic wrap (clingfilm) and twisting and tying the ends to create a sealed, compact cylinder. For stability and to prevent water seeping in during cooking, add a second layer of plastic wrap and then a layer of aluminum foil.

Place the cylinder in a steamer basket set over gently simmering water. Cover and steam for 1 hour, checking occasionally to make sure the water does not boil dry.

Prepare a bowl of ice water. Transfer the cylinder to the ice bath to stop the cooking process and preserve the shape.

Once cooled, unwrap the cylinder and cut it into thin slices using a mandoline (be sure to use the guard) or a very sharp knife. (You can also pan-fry them, to add a crunchy component to your sandwiches.)

assembly

Place the doughnuts flat on a work surface and carefully slice them open like a bagel. Spread some labneh on each. Top with a generous amount of the deli slices before closing.

Melt a little margarine in a skillet and fry the sandwich on both sides on medium-low heat, gently pressing them down, until caramelized and glossy.

Serve hot with a dusting of confectioners' (icing) sugar.

Breads

Bread has followed me through every chapter of my life. I grew up with soft white loaves, later discovered the strength of rustic crusts, and eventually learned how plants alone can build incredible character in dough. Flour, semolina, grains, and seeds all behave differently, and together they create doughs—I love those that stretch, rise, and take form under my hands. I find plant-based baking honors what these ingredients already know how to do.

The breads in this chapter are inspired by my travels and meant to spark curiosity. They range from Sesame *Khobz*, which reminds me of family tables (page 64), to Rye Bread full of warmth (page 67) to the softest of Glazed Sweet Potato Milk Buns (page 72). These breads will fill you with the comforting scent of a newly formed food memory and are made for sharing.

Sesame Khobz

Khobz (the Arabic word for "bread") is never missing at the dining table. There is an expression in Morocco that goes, "If you didn't eat bread, you didn't really eat."

The word can be used to describe any kind of bread, but in Morocco it usually refers only to this type—a round, springy loaf with enough crumb to perfectly soak up sauces and a thin crust to hold it together.

makes 4 small loaves

1 teaspoon active dry yeast
1⅓ cups (160 g) all-purpose (plain) flour
1 cup (170 g) fine semolina
1 teaspoon salt
½ cup (70 g) sesame seeds
sunflower oil, for rubbing

method

Put the yeast and 1 cup (250 ml) water into a stand mixer fitted with the hook attachment. Add the flour, semolina, and salt. Mix on low speed for 10 minutes.

Cover the dough in the bowl with a damp kitchen towel. Proof (prove) for 1 hour in a warm place, or until doubled in size.

On a clean work surface, divide the dough into 4 equal balls. Roll each piece until a smooth ball forms. Rub each ball with a little oil, then cover with a damp kitchen towel. Let rise for 30 minutes.

Preheat the oven to 400°F (200°C/Gas Mark 6). Line a baking sheet with parchment (baking) paper.

Put the sesame seeds into a large bowl. Using your palms, flatten each dough ball to a thickness of 1 inch (2.5 cm). One by one, place the flattened dough loaves on top of the sesame seeds to coat one side (a bench scraper comes in handy here), then place on the prepared baking sheet, sesame seed side up.

Cover the loaves with a dry kitchen towel and proof for 30–60 minutes. With the tip of your finger, press the dough: If it takes 2–3 seconds to spring back, it's ready. If it immediately springs back, it's underproofed. If the dough doesn't spring back at all, it has started overproofing and will probably collapse when baking—you'll need to start over in this case.

Bake the proofed loaves for 20–25 minutes, until golden brown.

Rye Bread

If I had to choose a bread to have every morning for breakfast, it would be this rye loaf. It is super rich, moist, and satisfying. Besides being tasty, rye bread is rich in fiber, which gives me a feeling of fullness, so I don't end up snacking shortly after breakfast. You can use this bread for many of the tartines in the next chapter.

makes 1 loaf

wet ingredients

2 tablespoons extra-virgin olive oil, plus extra for greasing and brushing
2 tablespoons maple syrup

dry ingredients

3 cups (380 g) bread flour
1 cup (100 g) rye flour
1¼ teaspoons salt
1 tablespoon active dry yeast
½ teaspoon ground cumin
½ teaspoon black pepper

method

Combine the wet ingredients and 1⅔ cups (400 ml) water in a bowl. Combine the dry ingredients in a separate bowl. Using a wooden spoon, slowly mix the wet ingredients into the dry until everything is well incorporated. Cover with a damp kitchen towel. Let rise at room temperature until doubled in size.

Meanwhile, grease an 11 × 4-inch (28 × 10-cm) loaf pan. Rub a little olive oil on your hands, then gently lift the dough from the bowl, stretching it upward from the middle and folding it over onto itself. Repeat this lift-stretch-fold sequence twice, or until the dough has a little tension. Transfer it to the prepared loaf pan. Brush with olive oil, cover with a damp kitchen towel, and set aside for 45 minutes, or until the dough rises to the rim of the pan.

Preheat the oven to 350°F (180°C/Gas Mark 4). Bake for 40–50 minutes, until golden brown.

Chef's Note: For a crunchy seed crust, soak a tablespoon each of sunflower, pumpkin, and poppy seeds in a cup of water before starting the bread dough. After placing the dough in the loaf pan, brush the top with water, and sprinkle the drained soaked seeds evenly overtop. Bake for 40–50 minutes, until golden brown.

Shokupan

Shokupan—the Japanese word for "bread" (or more precisely, "eating bread")—refers to a white, soft bread used for sandwiches. As a child, I was a massive fan of Japanese manga and anime. I spent hours in front of the TV watching *Doraemon, the Cosmic Cat*, who traveled back in time to solve everyday crises. He carried a four-dimensional "belly pocket" that produced gadgets and resources on demand—and one trick involved a slice of shokupan placed in a textbook to absorb all the knowledge. He then ate the bread to pass exams at school. I idolized him!

To make this bread exceptionally soft and airy, we use a Japanese technique called *yudane*. A portion of the flour is mixed with boiling water; the heat gelatinizes the starches, producing a tacky paste that holds water and improves dough extensibility. This simple additional step to the process makes a notable impact on texture and shelf life.

makes 1 loaf

yudane
- ½ cup (60 g) all-purpose (plain) flour

dough
- 2 cups (270 g) bread flour
- ¾ cup (180 ml) unsweetened soy milk
- 3½ tablespoons margarine, melted
- ¼ cup (50 g) raw sugar
- 2½ teaspoons active dry (fast-action dried) yeast
- 1 teaspoon salt
- sunflower oil, for greasing

glaze
- 3 tablespoons unsweetened soy milk
- 1 tablespoon maple syrup

method

yudane

In a heatproof bowl, pour ¼ cup (60 ml) boiling water over the flour and stir until it forms a sticky dough. Set aside for at least 20 minutes, or until cooled. Place the dough in the bowl of a stand mixer.

dough

Add all the dough ingredients to the yudane. Using a wooden spoon, mix until incorporated but still lumpy. Cover with a damp kitchen towel and let rest for 10 minutes.

Fit the stand mixer with the hook attachment and knead the dough on low speed for 15 minutes. Check the gluten development with the "windowpane" test: Tear off a small piece and stretch it gently until it becomes thin and translucent. If it stretches without tearing, the dough has sufficient gluten. If it breaks, knead for another 5 minutes.

Shape the dough into a ball and place it in a greased bowl. Cover with a damp kitchen towel and let rise at room temperature for 1–1½ hours, until doubled in size.

Transfer the dough to a clean work surface lightly dusted with flour. Knead it twice to remove the air. Divide it into 3 equal portions. Shape the portions into balls, and set aside.

Grease an 11 × 4-inch (28 by 10-cm) loaf pan. Place a dough ball onto a clean work surface and, using a rolling pin, roll it out into a square ½ inch (1 cm) thick. Fold two sides inward to create a rectangle, then roll it out lengthwise to the previous thickness. Starting along a shorter side of the rectangle and using your hands, roll the dough into a log and place it on a baking sheet, seam side down. Repeat with the remaining dough balls, placing them side by side in the prepared loaf pan, lightly touching.

glaze

Combine the ingredients in a small bowl.

assembly

Preheat the oven to 400°F (200°C/Gas Mark 6).

Brush the dough generously with the glaze. Cover with a damp clean kitchen towel. Set aside for 45–60 minutes, until it rises to the rim of the loaf pan.

Brush the dough with more glaze. Reduce the oven temperature to 350°F (180°C/Gas Mark 4) and bake for 25 minutes, or until golden brown. If the crust is browning too quickly, loosely cover the loaf with aluminum foil to prevent it from hardening.

Potato Buns with Black Cumin Seeds

These buns began as part of the weekend rituals Marc and I built long before I became a chef. When I was still working as an engineer, we'd grill burgers by the lake and make every component ourselves. Cooking for him and for friends was an early escape from my desk job, and the place where my confidence in the kitchen slowly took shape. We tried countless bread recipes, but I always came back to the softness of a potato bun—somewhere between an Eastern European braided bread and a classic potato roll. This version stays true to that. The black cumin seeds bring a peppery, slightly bitter edge that cuts the sweetness of the dough and adds texture and contrast.

makes 8 buns

- 1 russet potato, unpeeled
- 3½ tablespoons margarine, melted
- 1 cup (250 ml) unsweetened soy milk
- juice of ½ lemon
- 1 tablespoon chia seeds
- 1 tablespoon active dry yeast
- 3 cups (400 g) bread flour
- 1 tablespoon maple syrup
- 1½ teaspoons salt

glaze

- 3½ tablespoons unsweetened oat milk
- 3½ tablespoons sunflower oil
- 2 tablespoons maple syrup
- 4 teaspoons Dijon mustard

to finish

- ¼ cup (30 g) black cumin seeds
- 1 teaspoon flaky salt

method

Preheat the oven to 400°F (200°C/Gas Mark 6).

Bake the unpeeled potato for 40–50 minutes, until soft. Remove from the oven and, once cool enough to handle, peel off the potato skin.

Using a spatula, pass the flesh through a fine-mesh strainer (sieve). In a small saucepan, combine ⅔ cup (150 g) of the potato puree and the margarine. Heat over low heat until the margarine has melted.

In a small bowl, combine the soy milk and lemon juice. Let sit for 5 minutes.

Meanwhile, blend the chia seeds into a fine powder. Pass them through a fine-mesh strainer into a bowl. Drizzle 2 tablespoons water over the chia powder and mix well.

In the bowl of a stand mixer fitted with the hook attachment, combine the chia paste, soy milk mixture, and yeast. Stir to combine. Add the potato puree, bread flour, maple syrup, and salt. Knead on low speed for 10 minutes.

Transfer the dough to a lightly greased bowl. Cover with a damp kitchen towel. Let rise for 45 minutes, or until doubled in size.

glaze
Meanwhile, whisk together the ingredients in a bowl until well combined. Set aside.

assembly
Place the dough on a clean work surface and use a bench scraper to portion it into 8 (4-oz/110-g) pieces. Cover with a damp kitchen towel to prevent them from drying out.

Shape each dough piece into a ball, either by pressing it against your work surface and moving your hand in a circular motion or by rolling it between two hands.

Place the dough balls on a baking sheet lined with parchment paper, lightly touching one another. Brush with the glaze. Cover with a damp kitchen towel and let rise in a warm place for 30 minutes, or until doubled in size.

Preheat a convection oven to 350°F (180°C/Gas Mark 4).

Brush the buns again with the glaze. Bake for 20 minutes, or until golden brown. Remove from the oven and glaze once more. Sprinkle with the cumin seeds and flaky salt.

Glazed Sweet Potato Milk Buns

Potato buns are my first choice for pairing with a smashed patty on a burger. When I created the burger menu for our cocktail bar, our intention was to serve a version of the soft potato bun—but after several tests, I decided to develop a more decadent dough.

Because we don't use eggs, I needed another way to enrich the dough, which is why we ended up using baked sweet potatoes. I spent a lot of time researching Japanese milk bread and classic American potato buns to arrive at this recipe, which we now use for hot dogs at KLE, burgers at DAR, and for sharing in the center of the table at home.

makes 20 mini buns

sweet potato milk buns
- 1 sweet potato, unpeeled
- ½ cup (120 ml) unsweetened oat milk
- 3½ tablespoons margarine, plus extra for greasing
- 2¾ cups (340 g) all-purpose (plain) flour
- 3 tablespoons raw sugar
- 2½ teaspoons active dry yeast
- ¼ teaspoon salt

glaze
- ⅓ cup (75 ml) maple syrup
- 3 tablespoons Sriracha
- 1 tablespoon extra-virgin olive oil
- 1 teaspoon lemon juice

to serve
- ⅔ cup (50 g) store-bought fried onions

method

sweet potato milk buns
Preheat the oven to 400°F (200°C/Gas Mark 6). Bake the sweet potato for 40–50 minutes, until soft. Remove from the oven and set aside until cool enough to handle. Peel off the skin.

Use a spatula to pass the potato flesh through a fine-mesh strainer (sieve). In a small saucepan, combine ⅔ cup (150 g) of the potato puree, the oat milk, and margarine. Heat over low heat until the margarine has melted.

Place the potato mixture in a stand mixer fitted with the hook attachment. Add the flour, raw sugar, dry yeast, and salt. Knead on low speed for 10 minutes. Transfer the dough to a lightly greased bowl and cover with a damp clean kitchen towel. Let rise for 45 minutes, or until doubled in size.

glaze
Meanwhile, whisk together the glaze ingredients in a bowl. Set aside.

assembly
Line a 10-inch (25-cm) square baking sheet with parchment (baking) paper. Place the dough on a clean work surface and apply pressure to release the trapped air. Using a bench scraper, portion the dough into 20 (1-oz/30-g) pieces. Cover with a damp kitchen towel to prevent them from drying out.

Shape each dough piece into a ball. Place on the prepared baking sheet, lightly touching one another. Brush with the glaze. Cover with a damp kitchen towel and let rise in a warm place for 30 minutes, or until doubled in size.

Preheat a convection oven to 350°F (180°C/Gas Mark 4).

Brush the buns again with the glaze. Place the baking sheet on the middle rack of the oven and bake for 10 minutes. Brush again with the glaze. Bake for another 15 minutes, or until golden. Remove from the oven, glaze once more, and top with the fried onions. Serve warm.

Chef's Note: To use these as burger buns, divide the dough into 6 (3½-oz/100-g) portions for larger rolls.

Ramp Focaccia

Making focaccia always quiets the room and my mind—the slow waits, the soft shaping, the joy of tearing into a warm, dimpled cloud. I first imagined this focaccia with ramps (wild garlic), but their season is brief, so we tried topping the dough with chopped sauerkraut just before baking—and got fantastic results.

This recipe employs a technique called "coil fold," which involves lifting the center of the dough with wet hands, allowing it to stretch and fold over itself, and then rotating the bowl to repeat the process until the dough gains tension and coils nicely.

serves 8

- 1 teaspoon active dry yeast
- 3⅔ cups (500 g) bread flour
- 2 teaspoons salt
- 2 teaspoons extra-virgin olive oil, for drizzling and greasing
- 1 tablespoon coarse semolina, plus extra for dusting
- 1 teaspoon flaky salt
- 20 ramp (wild garlic) leaves (see above) or ⅔ cup (140 g) sauerkraut

method

In the bowl of a stand mixer fitted with the hook attachment, stir the yeast into 1½ cups (365 ml) lukewarm water. Add the flour and knead for 4 minuteson low speed. Add the salt and knead for another 2 minutes. Let rest for 10 minutes.

Oil your hands generously with olive oil and begin a set of coil fold. Set the dough aside for 20 minutes. Repeat the coil fold and rest process twice more.

After the last fold, place the dough in a greased bowl and cover with a damp kitchen towel. Let rise for 45 minutes, or until doubled in size.

Lightly dust a clean work surface with coarse semolina. Gently tip the dough onto it, keeping as much air in it as possible. Fold the dough onto itself until the surface is smooth. Coat the dough with the semolina. Carefully transfer it to a 12 × 9-inch (30 × 22-cm) baking dish brushed with olive oil. Gently stretch the dough to fill the baking dish. If it feels too tight or resistant to the stretch, let it rest for 5 minutes. (Sometimes a dough needs to relax before flattening it.) Cover with a damp kitchen towel and let rise for 2 hours, or until doubled in size and bubbly.

Preheat the oven to 450°F (230°C/Gas Mark 8).

Drizzle the proofed focaccia dough with the olive oil and dimple the top using your oiled fingertips. Sprinkle with the flaky salt, followed by a generous amount of olive oil. Rub the ramp (wild garlic) leaves (or sauerkraut) in olive oil and lay over the surface, applying gentle pressure so they stick to the dough.

Bake for 10–15 minutes, until golden brown and the bottom sounds hollow when tapped.

Chef's Note: Timers are a very useful tool in the kitchen, especially when shaping breads like focaccia and sourdough.

Flatbread with Apple Honey

Meloui is one of the dishes that anchors me most deeply to childhood. This flaky, indulgent flatbread from the Maghreb wasn't something we had often at home (its shaping takes time and patience), but whenever we visited family in Morocco, I could count on having it every morning. That generosity is typical of Moroccan hospitality, and those breakfasts felt like pure luxury. Today, whenever I feel homesick, working the dough takes me back there instantly. The smell of semolina toasting in the pan and the sensation of stretching the dough into a thin, translucent sheet echo the movements I watched in the hands of older relatives. Working the dough properly takes practice, but the reward is unmistakable.

This flatbread is flexible enough for sweet or savory fillings and rich enough to stand on its own. The process is fairly hands-on but the repetition is part of its pleasure. Once cooked, serve it warm with apple honey or maple syrup and a little melted margarine or olive oil.

---

makes 10 flatbreads

dough

5 cups (600 g) all-purpose (plain) flour
1½ cups (250 g) fine semolina
2 teaspoons sugar
1 teaspoon salt
¼ teaspoon active dry yeast
sunflower oil, for rubbing

to shape

3½ tablespoons margarine, softened, plus 1 teaspoon for frying
¼ cup (50 g) coarse semolina

to serve

Apple Honey (page 265) or maple syrup
melted margarine or extra-virgin olive oil, for drizzling

method

dough

Combine all the dough ingredients in the bowl of a stand mixer fitted with a hook attachment. Gradually pour in 2⅓ cups (540 ml) lukewarm water and mix for 5 minutes.

Lightly oil the dough with the sunflower oil. Cover with a damp clean kitchen towel and let rest for 30 minutes at room temperature. (I often prepare the dough the night before and rest it in the refrigerator overnight. This way, the dough is ready to be stretched the next morning.)

Pinch the dough into 10 smooth balls. Cover with the kitchen towel and let rest for another 20 minutes.

to shape

Meanwhile, prepare two small bowls: one with the softened margarine and one with the coarse semolina.

On a well-oiled work surface, press each dough ball as thin as possible using the palm of your hand. Brush the discs with a little margarine, then stretch each with the tips of your fingers against the work surface, until the dough transforms into a thin, translucent "veil." Brush with more margarine and sprinkle over a little of the coarse semolina.

Fold two sides of a dough piece inward, sprinkle a little more semolina on top, and then roll the dough into a coil. Turn the coil on its side and flatten with your hand. Let rest for 15 minutes while you shape the remaining flatbreads. Make sure all the coils are covered in fat so that no crust is created.

Melt 1 teaspoon of margarine in a cast-iron skillet over medium heat. Flatten the flatbreads again so they are ¼ inch (5 mm) thick. Add the flatbreads and fry for 8–10 minutes on each side, until golden brown and cooked through.

to serve

Serve warm, drizzled with the apple honey (or maple syrup) and melted margarine (or olive oil).

Tartines

For years, I thought of tartines as quick, light snacks—something I'd never choose over a proper meal. That changed during an Italian wedding where I was only a guest, not the one cooking. Tartines were arranged on beautiful stands and treated with intention. Suddenly, this simple concept of bread plus toppings felt both expressive and expansive. A tartine can be breakfast in seconds or a centerpiece at a party! It can be rustic or polished, depending entirely on how you build it.

The tartines in this chapter come from that memory. They are built to feel generous and relaxed, the kind of food you want to set out in the center of the table for friends. And best of all, a tartine doesn't need rules! You can choose a sturdy sourdough or a soft focaccia, load it with vegetables, spreads, or something bright and pickled, and it becomes whatever you want it to be—casual or elegant, hearty or delicate.

These recipes are full of color and texture and meant to be enjoyed however you like. When a tartine lands just right, it feels effortless, even though every ingredient carries its own story. It's now one of my favorite things to serve.

Avocado, Lemon, Toasted Hemp Seeds, and Labneh Tartine

30'

I was confused the first time I saw avocado toast. I had graduated from college and was watching a Nigella Lawson video on a quick breakfast toast that started with familiar ingredients: ripe tomatoes and mashed chickpeas. Then she began smashing an avocado and spreading spoonfuls of it on rye toast. That shook me. Honestly, it didn't look at all appetizing to me, but I trusted Nigella unconditionally and tried it. I instantly fell in love with it. This variation on the classic is equally delicious.

serves 2

1 lemon
2 tablespoons hemp seeds
extra-virgin olive oil, for frying and drizzling
2 slices Rye Bread (page 67)
2 tablespoons Labneh (page 262)
1 ripe avocado
flaky salt
1 tablespoon finely chopped cilantro (coriander)

method

Grate the lemon zest into a bowl and set aside. Peel the lemon, remove the white pith, and cut out sections using a paring knife. Cut each section into thirds.

Toast the hemp seeds in a dry nonstick skillet. Set aside.

Add a little oil to the same skillet. Toast both sides of the rye bread slices until golden brown.

Spread the labneh onto the toast. Halve, pit (stone), and thinly slice the avocado. Fan the slices on top of each toast. Top with the lemon pieces. Drizzle with olive oil, then sprinkle with flaky salt. Finish with the lemon zest, toasted hemp seeds, and cilantro (coriander).

Hummus
and Caramelized Onion Spread on Sesame Khobz

Sometimes when brunch is especially busy at DAR, I forget to feed myself. When the rush has passed, I usually crave a slice of comfort—and this trusted tartine never disappoints.

Daghmira is a concentrated Moroccan onion paste made by slowly reducing finely chopped onions until caramelized, which I've brightened here with prunes. Its deep and tangy notes complement hummus's lemony-tahini richness, and its dense, spreadable texture soaks into the khobz's crumb, while the bread's crust provides needed bite. If prunes are not available, I recommend using raisins or dried apricots.

serves 2

hummus

- 2¾ cups (500 g) dried chickpeas, soaked overnight, or 5 cups (800 g) cooked chickpeas
- 1 teaspoon baking soda (bicarbonate of soda)
- 3 cloves garlic
- sunflower oil, for confit
- 1½ teaspoons salt
- ¼ teaspoon ground cumin
- ½ cup (120 g) tahini
- 2 tablespoons extra-virgin olive oil
- juice of 1 lemon

daghmira

- 1¼ cup (250 g) prunes, pitted (stoned) and quartered
- 1 tablespoon sunflower oil
- 1–2 white onions (250 g), finely sliced
- 1 cinnamon stick
- 1 teaspoon salt
- 1 teaspoon ras el hanout
- 2 strands saffron

to serve

- 1 Sesame Khobz (page 64)
- 1 tablespoon sesame seeds or chopped almonds, toasted

method

hummus

Place the dried or canned chickpeas and baking soda (bicarbonate of soda) in a large saucepan, cover generously with water, and simmer for 1 hour, or until soft. (When using canned chickpeas, I still cook them to achieve a silky texture.)

Meanwhile, place the garlic in a small saucepan and cover with sunflower oil. Bring to a gentle simmer over medium heat. Reduce the heat to low and cook for 10–15 minutes, until the garlic is soft but not colored. Remove from the heat and let cool.

Drain the chickpeas and let cool. In a blender, combine the chickpeas, confit garlic cloves, 2 tablespoons of the confit oil, and the remaining ingredients. Add ⅓ cup (75 ml) of ice water, adding more as needed until the hummus reaches your desired consistency.

daghmira

Soak the prunes in 1 cup (250 ml) boiling water and set aside.

Meanwhile, heat the sunflower oil over medium-low heat. Add the onions, cinnamon, and salt and sauté for 30 minutes, or until the onions are softened and dark caramelized. Stir the onions occasionally to prevent them from burning.

Add the remaining ingredients, including the prune soaking water, and cover. Cook over low heat for 30 minutes, stirring occasionally. Add a tablespoon of water to deglaze the pan if it dries out.

Transfer the daghmira to a heatproof bowl. Let cool to room temperature.

assembly

Slice and toast the khobz. Spread a generous spoon of the hummus on the cut side of the khobz, creating a well in the center. Fill with daghmira and top with the sesame seeds (or toasted almonds).

Chef's Note: Garlic confit is a staple ingredient in our kitchens. I recommend cooking big batches and storing them in the refrigerator for up to 2 months—just make sure the cloves remain covered by the oil. Use the oil for pan-frying and the cloves for adding a sweet garlic note to your recipes.

Pea-sto
with Pickled Carrots and Togarashi

This "pea-sto" tartine started as a bright, reliable stand-in for avocadoes when they're out of season. It features a savory spread of peas, herbs, capers, and lemon, but the pickled carrots are the defining element—its pickling liquid of nori, rice vinegar, soy, and maple syrup brings clean, sushi-like notes and a vivid color. Adding a few drops of liquid smoke deepens the flavor and gives it a warm smokiness that balances the entire act.

Togarashi is a Japanese spice blend of chili, citrus peel, and sesame and appears throughout the book as a signature seasoning. My variation with kimchi brings a subtle heat and depth that enhances the sweetness of the peas and fresh herbs.

serves 2

pickled carrots
2 sheets nori
1½ teaspoons salt
½ cup (120 ml) rice vinegar
¼ cup (60 ml) soy sauce
1 tablespoon maple syrup
4 drops liquid smoke
2 large carrots, shaved into long ribbons

pea-sto
2 cups (300 g) peas
8 large mint leaves
8 large basil leaves
2 cloves garlic
2 tablespoons extra-virgin olive oil
2 tablespoons lemon juice
2 teaspoons capers
1 tablespoon nutritional yeast
½ teaspoon Espelette pepper or Moroccan cayenne pepper
½ teaspoon salt, plus extra to taste

assembly
2 slices Rye Bread (page 67)
Kimchi Togarashi (page 258), for sprinkling
chopped parsley, tarragon, mint, or basil, for sprinkling (optional)

method

pickled carrots
Place all the ingredients except the carrots in a large saucepan. Add 2 cups (470 ml) water and bring to a boil over medium heat. Remove from the heat, add the carrots, and set aside to cool completely.

Store the pickled carrots and pickling liquid in an airtight container in the refrigerator for up to 1 week.

pea-sto
In a food processor, combine all the ingredients and process to a pesto-like consistency. Season with salt and hot pepper.

assembly
Toast the rye bread, then place a slice on each of two plates. Spread with a generous amount of the pea-sto. Top with the pickled carrots and sprinkle with the kimchi togarashi. Finish with fresh herbs, if you like.

Cherry Tomatoes and Charred Onions on Pumpernickel

Because pumpernickel tends to be thinly sliced, we build this tartine in layers. I recommend eating it with a fork and a knife to avoid a mess. The sharpness comes primarily from the cheese spread, although you can also finish it with a squeeze of lemon.

Tomatoes and onions are a classic pairing—the sweetness and acidity of the tomato complement the bitter charred onions. The pumpernickel bread is dense so can hold all the juices, but it also adds an earthy and tangy profile thanks to its fermentation.

---

serves 2

baked cherry tomatoes

3½ ounces (100 g) cherry tomatoes
extra-virgin olive oil, for drizzling
salt and black pepper
1 teaspoon dried oregano

charred onions

1 tablespoon sunflower oil
1 white onion, slice into ½-inch (1-cm) thick rings
2 tablespoons sherry vinegar

assembly

1 beefsteak tomato, thinly sliced
extra-virgin olive oil, for drizzling
salt and black pepper
1 cup (240 g) Cheese spread (page 105)
6 slices pumpernickel bread
½ stalk celery, thinly sliced
finely chopped chives, dill, tarragon, and chervil, for sprinkling
flaky salt

method

baked cherry tomatoes

Preheat the oven to 210°F (100°C/Gas Mark ¼).

Place the cherry tomatoes on a baking sheet. Drizzle with olive oil. Season with salt, pepper, and the oregano. Bake for 10–15 minutes, until slightly shriveled.

charred onions

Heat the sunflower oil in a skillet over medium-high heat. Add the onion rings and sear for 10 minutes. Carefully turn them over and brown for 7 minutes. Deglaze the pan with the vinegar. Carefully transfer the onions to a plate.

assembly

Season the tomato slices with olive oil, salt, and pepper.

Spread the cheese spread on 2 slices of pumpernickel. Top with fresh tomato slices and charred onion rings, then with the baked cherry tomatoes and celery.

Repeat with two more layers. Garnish with the fresh herbs and finish with flaky salt.

Fig, Cashew-Miso Spread, and Orange Reduction Tartine

30'

This flavor combination always lifts my mood, the fresh figs taking me back to a time when my mom and I would pluck them from our neighbor's tree. But my fondest memory of that time is chasing after my brother, who disliked figs, with my sticky fig hands.

serves 2

cashew-miso spread

¾ cup (100 g) cashew nuts, soaked overnight
2 tablespoons aged red miso
¼ teaspoon salt
1½ teaspoons apple cider vinegar

orange reduction

1 cup (250 ml) orange juice
1 tablespoon extra-virgin olive oil

assembly

6 figs, sliced (see Note)
2 slices rustic seed bread
1 tablespoon balsamic vinegar
⅓ cup (50 g) walnuts, toasted

method

cashew-miso spread

Drain the cashews, then rinse them under running water. In a small blender, combine the nuts with the remaining ingredients and 2 tablespoons water. Blend until smooth.

orange reduction

Pour the orange juice into a small saucepan and reduce over medium heat by three-quarters. Whisk in the olive oil until emulsified.

assembly

Spread the cashew-miso spread over the bread slices. Fan the figs on top. Drizzle with the orange reduction and balsamic vinegar. Top with the toasted walnuts.

Chef's Note: If your figs are unripe, pan-fry them with a little brown sugar to caramelize them and soften the flesh.

Focaccia with Taktouka and Crumbled "Feta"

Taktouka is a Moroccan cooked salad built with charred bell peppers, ripe tomatoes, and garlic and seasoned with warm spices. It's frequently enjoyed as a warm dip, but you also can serve it in a bowl in the center of the table, with the "feta" sprinkled on top alongside, as a side or as individual servings.

serves 2

- 4 red bell peppers
- ¼ cup (60 ml) extra-virgin olive oil, plus extra to taste
- 2 cloves garlic, minced
- 2 teaspoons sweet paprika
- 1 teaspoon ground cumin
- ½ teaspoon black pepper
- 4–5 tomatoes, finely chopped
- ⅓ cup (25 g) chopped parsley, plus extra for sprinkling
- 1 teaspoon salt, or to taste
- 2 teaspoons raw sugar, or to taste
- 2 slices Ramp Focaccia (page 75), pita bread, Lebanese flatbread (*manakish*), or Persian bread (*barbari*)
- ½ cup (75 g) Feta-Style Cheese (page 263)
- 1 tablespoon cilantro (coriander) leaves

method

Preheat the oven to 500°F (250°C/Gas Mark 10) or preheat a charcoal grill.

Place the bell peppers on a baking sheet lined with aluminum foil and roast for 10–20 minutes. (Alternatively, place on the charcoal grill, turning every 5 minutes, or until charred all over.) Transfer the peppers to a bowl and cover with plastic wrap (clingfilm). Let steam for 10 minutes. Peel and discard the skins from the peppers. Remove the stems and seeds, then halve and finely chop. Set aside.

Heat the olive oil in a nonstick skillet over medium heat.

Add the garlic and sauté for 2 minutes, or until golden brown. Add the spices and toast for 1 minute, or until fragrant. Add the bell peppers, tomatoes, and parsley. Simmer over medium heat for 30 minutes. Adjust the seasoning with salt, sugar, or olive oil to taste.

Toast the bread and place on serving plates. Top with the taktouka and crumbled "feta." Sprinkle with parsley and cilantro (coriander).

Sweet Potato Muhammara, Green Asparagus, and Toasted Sunflower Seeds

This tartine was built around the simple pleasure of grilled green asparagus. It quickly became a guest favorite. Pairing it here with DAR's sweet potato *muhammara* turns it into a completely plant-based dish with real depth. Traditional muhammara relies on walnuts and sweet peppers, but using sweet potatoes gives the spread a natural sweetness, a velvety texture, and a beautiful color—all while using produce our farmers can harvest nearly year-round. Sunflower seeds add warmth and richness, making the recipe accessible and satisfying and still nut-free. Easy to assemble, rooted in seasonal vegetables, and full of contrast, what more could you ask for?

---

serves 2

sweet potato muhammara

2 large sweet potatoes (about 1 pound/500 g)
2 onions, peeled
2 cloves garlic
1 red pepperoncino or serrano chile, seeded
7 sprigs thyme, leaves only
¼ cup (1 g) sunflower seeds
2 tablespoons white vinegar
2 tablespoons pomegranate molasses
1 tablespoon extra-virgin olive oil
1 teaspoon smoked paprika
2 teaspoons ground cumin
1½ teaspoons salt
¼ teaspoon ground fennel seeds

asparagus

olive oil, for grilling and finishing
6 asparagus, woody stems trimmed (see Note)
flaky salt
zest and juice of 1 lime

assembly

2 slices rustic bread
½ teaspoon za'atar
2 tablespoons sunflower seeds, toasted

method

sweet potato muhammara

Preheat the oven to 400°F (200°C/Gas Mark 8). Wrap the sweet potatoes, onions, garlic, and chile in aluminum foil and place on a baking sheet. Roast for 40 minutes, or until softened and golden brown. Set aside to cool slightly.

Once the sweet potatoes are cool enough to handle, peel them. Combine all the remaining ingredients in a blender or food processor and process to a spreadable consistency.

asparagus

Lightly grease a ridged grill pan and heat over high heat until smoking hot. If the asparagus is very thick, blanch it in boiling water for 1–2 minutes. Immediately transfer to ice water to stop the cooking. Pat dry with paper towel. Grill the asparagus on one side for 3 minutes, or until lightly charred. Turn and grill for another 3 minutes.

Place the asparagus on a plate and season with flaky salt, olive oil, and the lime zest and juice. Cut the asparagus stalks into thirds, if you like.

assembly

Grill the bread on the grill pan, then transfer to a cutting board. Spread sweet potato muhammara on each slice. Top with the charred asparagus and za'atar. Sprinkle with the sunflower seeds.

Collard Greens–Mustard Mashed Potato Tartine

This tartine best represents the Swiss-German flavor combination of potatoes, mustard, and collard greens. The ingredients are almost always available, which means I can enjoy this dish perennially.

Our farmers usually bring us collard greens in big quantities, and because they are strong plants, they can be harvested even when the snow starts for the season. This gives the farmers a source of income even when the overall production in the fields decreases because of the drop in temperature.

---

serves 2

collard greens

- 9 ounces (250 g) collard greens (spring greens) or Swiss chard, stems and leaves separated
- 1 tablespoon sunflower oil
- 3½ ounces (100 g) smoked tofu, coarsely grated
- 1 red onion, finely diced
- 1 teaspoon salt
- 1½ teaspoons ground fennel seeds
- 3 tablespoons BBQ sauce
- zest and juice of 1 lemon

mustard mashed potatoes

- 3 starchy potatoes (12 oz/350 g), cut into 1-inch (2.5-cm) cubes
- 2 tablespoons margarine, melted
- 3 tablespoons whole-grain mustard
- 1 tablespoon hot mustard
- 1 tablespoon extra-virgin olive oil
- 1 tablespoon maple syrup
- ¼ teaspoon salt
- ¼ teaspoon black pepper

assembly

- 1 small ciabatta loaf
- ¼ cup (50 g) store-bought fried onions
- 1 gherkin, chopped
- 3 sprigs dill
- pickle (gherkin) juice, for drizzling (optional)
- grated horseradish or chili sauce (optional)

method

collard greens

Coarsely chop the collard green (or spring greens or Swiss chard) leaves. Thinly slice the stems.

Heat the sunflower oil in a skillet over medium-high heat. Add the smoked tofu and sauté for 5 minutes, or until browned. Reduce the heat to medium. Add the onion and salt. Sauté for another 7 minutes, or until the onion dice are softened and starting to color.

Stir in the greens, ground fennel seeds, and BBQ sauce. Cook for another 10 minutes, or until the greens are wilted. Remove from the heat, then season with the lemon zest and juice.

mustard mashed potatoes

Place the potatoes in a large saucepan of cold salted water. Bring to a boil over medium-high heat, then boil the potatoes for 20 minutes, or until tender. Drain the potatoes, transfer to a bowl, and mash with a fork. Stir in the melted margarine, both mustards, the olive oil, and maple syrup. Season with the salt and pepper.

assembly

Toast the ciabatta, then spread with the mashed potatoes.
Cover with the collard greens.
Top with the fried onions, pickles (gherkins) and sprigs of dill.
Drizzle with a little pickle (gherkin) juice and add a little horseradish, if you like.

Bites and Nibbles

Before I became a chef, I'd spend my free hours cooking for friends in my apartment. The table was always covered with little things to taste and whatever I had been experimenting with that week. I didn't have technique yet, but I had curiosity, and those evenings taught me how powerful these small dishes can be. It reminded me that flavor doesn't need to be complicated or heavy to make an impression; it just needs care.

The recipes in this chapter are meant to be fun, generous, and easy to share. To my mind, small bites should be a pocket of flavor—something that impresses in just a couple of mouthfuls and compels you to want another. Some, such as Watermelon Shiso Kimchi (page 102) are built on bright flavors while others, such as Gem Lettuce Hearts with Mandarin and Poppy Seeds (page 101) or the Vegan Cheese-Filled Piquillo Peppers (page 105), lean on crunch and creaminess. I like to have a variety of tastes and textures—some to be eaten by hand, some with a spoon, and even little shot glasses or mini mugs for a warm spiced soup in winter.

Fruit and Vegetable Platter with Tahini Dip and Labneh

Sometimes you simply want to snack on something fresh and crunchy. I prefer the specific veggies I use here for crudites, because they stay juicy and crunchy over time. To keep the fruit and veggies from oxidizing, I sprinkle them with a little lemon juice and serve them on crushed ice. I chose these two dips because they are simple yet super indulgent and perfect to share with unannounced guests.

serves 6

fruit and vegetable platter

1 apple, cored and cut into wedges
1 pear, cored and cut into wedges
1 kohlrabi or jicama, cut into batons
1 Belgian endive, trimmed and leaves separated
1 handful sugar snap peas

tahini dip

1 cup (220 g) tahini
1 tablespoon pomegranate molasses
1 tablespoon date syrup
2 tablespoons soy sauce
2 tablespoons lemon juice

assembly

Labneh (page 262)

method

fruit and vegetable platter

Arrange the fruit and vegetables on a serving tray or place them in separate bowls.

tahini dip

Whisk all the ingredients in a bowl. Transfer to a large shallow serving bowl. Using a spoon, make a swirl in the center.

assembly

Plate the labneh in the same manner as the tahini dip. Place both dips next to the platter.

Gem Lettuce Hearts with Mandarin and Poppy Seeds

30'

Lettuce hearts are such an underrated ingredient. Often relegated to boring salads, I consider them the perfect canvas for small snacks. Super crunchy and sturdy, they can carry flavor with ease and hide surprises between their layers. My brother and I used to snack on them when we were left alone at home, dipping them into a simple vinaigrette. I sometimes prefer to snack on salad hearts rather than potato chips (crisps).

This recipe is a little more elaborate, but still simple and equally delicious. Since tasting peanut dipping sauce in Vietnam, I always stock peanut butter in my seasoning cabinet and use it in dressings. Everyone knows peanut butter and jelly is a great combo, so for this salad I made a peanut butter sauce to go with the mandarin sections for the fruity component. The poppy seeds bring a crunchy texture, color, and nuttiness.

---

serves 6

dressing

2½ tablespoons sugar-free crunchy peanut butter
3 tablespoons mirin
1½ tablespoons soy sauce
½ teaspoon salt
zest of 1 mandarin

salad

2 baby gem lettuce hearts or Belgian endives, cut into 6 wedges
1 tablespoon poppy seeds
2 mandarins, sectioned
pinch of flaky salt

method

dressing

In a glass jar with a lid, combine all the ingredients. Add 1 tablespoon water and shake well. The dressing should have a honey-like consistency. If needed, add another tablespoon of water to loosen it up.

salad

Arrange the lettuce hearts (or endives), cut side up, on a plate. Drizzle over the dressing, then sprinkle with the poppy seeds. Tuck a few mandarin sections between the leaves of each lettuce wedge. Finish with flaky salt.

Watermelon Shiso Kimchi

Watermelon is not often available in Switzerland, but some of our farmers—such as Salvador Garibay or Christian and Leo from SoLaWi (short for *Solidarische Landwirtschaft*, or "community-supported agriculture," in which consumers commit to buying a share of a farm's harvest in advance)—always plant it for us. My childhood summers were filled with watermelon, but now it's a luxury, so we serve it almost untouched.

This was one of the first snacks on the tasting menu at restaurant KLE. It's a refreshing, light yet complex bite. We wait for the watermelon to be perfectly ripe and add only a couple of flattering ingredients. Shiso is highly aromatic and herbal, while kimchi is acidic and spicy; both complement the juicy sweetness of the fruit.

serves 6

½ watermelon
juice of 1 lemon
2 tablespoons extra-virgin olive oil
12 shiso leaves
flaky salt
1 tablespoon Kimchi Togarashi (page 258) or kimchi powder (see Note)

method

Remove and discard the watermelon rind. Cut the flesh into 12 batons. You can freeze the scraps for juicing or salad dressings.

In a bowl, whisk together the lemon juice and olive oil. Toss the watermelon pieces in the marinade, making sure they are coated. Let sit for 5 minutes.

Place a watermelon baton in the center of a shiso leaf, wrapping the leaf around the melon like a taco shell. Crush some flaky salt on top and sprinkle generously with kimchi togarashi (or kimchi powder).

Chef's Note: Kimchi powder is made from dried, ground kimchi and delivers concentrated heat, tang, and savory depth. It is available at well-stocked Asian supermarkets and from specialty spice retailers.

Vegan Cheese-Filled Piquillo Peppers

30′

One of the most popular tapas in Spanish bars, this is a simple snack that you can prepare in advance and store in the refrigerator. I love using the preserving oil from piquillo peppers for focaccia, salad dressings, or pasta, and always keep a jar in the refrigerator. These peppers are traditionally filled with products from animal origin, but here we make a plant-based version.

---

makes 12 peppers

cheese spread
2 cups (450 g) Labneh (page 262)
2 tablespoons extra-virgin olive oil
zest of 1 lemon
1 bunch chives, finely chopped, plus extra for garnish
¼ teaspoon black pepper

piquillo peppers
1 (14-oz/400-g) can piquillo peppers in oil, drained
extra-virgin olive oil, for drizzling
flaky salt, to finish
toasted bread

method

cheese spread
Combine all the ingredients in a bowl. Transfer to a pastry (piping) bag and store in the refrigerator until needed.

piquillo peppers
Open each pepper and pipe in the cheese about three-quarters full. Finish with a drizzle of olive oil, chives, and a pinch of flaky salt. Place on top of small slices of toasted bread.

Panko-Crusted Stuffed Olives

30'

Crisp on the outside, juicy and briny in the middle, with a soft, creamy filling that melts just enough to feel indulgent without being heavy—the contrast of textures makes these stuffed olives o satisfying. Best of all, they come together with very little effort: pipe, coat, and fry.

Jumbo olives work best here, giving you plenty of room for the filling and a more balanced bite. If unavailable, simply fry standard olives and pipe the cheese on top just before serving.

makes 24 stuffed olives

1 (8-oz/227-g) jar jumbo olives, drained
⅓ cup (80 g) Cheese spread (page 105)
¼ teaspoon crushed red pepper
sunflower or vegetable oil, for frying
⅔ cup (80 g) all-purpose (plain) flour, plus extra for dusting
salt and black pepper
2 cups (150 g) panko bread crumbs

method

Place the olives on a baking sheet lined with paper towels. In a bowl, combine the cheese spread and crushed red pepper. Fill a pastry (piping) bag with the spread, then pipe it into the olives. Refrigerate the olives until needed.

Heat about 1½ inches (3 cm) of oil in a small deep saucepan over medium heat to 350°F (180°C).

In a bowl, combine the flour and a pinch each of salt and pepper. Gradually whisk ⅔ cup (150 ml) of water into the flour until you have a smooth batter. Put the panko crumbs into a bowl.

Dust each olive lightly with flour. Using two forks, dip the olives into the batter one at a time, making sure they are completely coated. Transfer to the panko and gently roll between your hands so the crumbs adhere well and the olives are rounded.

Gently lower the olives into the oil and deep-fry for 1–2 minutes, until the panko turns golden. Avoid over-frying them to prevent the filling from leaking into the oil. Using a slotted spoon, transfer the olives to a paper towel–lined plate. Season with a little salt to finish.

Serve immediately with toothpicks.

Loaded Spanish Chips

This snack is perfect served with vermouth or a pre-lunch aperitif. In Spain, we have *la hora del vermut*, or "vermouth time." Guests typically stand around a high table or at the bar, sharing small bites and drinking vermouth on the rocks.

This tapa balances salt, acidity, and spice to match the sweet, bitter, and herbal notes of a vermouth or aperitif. It's finished with salsa Espinaler—a classic Catalan hot sauce known for its sharp, savory kick.

serves 6

salsa Espinaler

- 1 cup (250 ml) white wine vinegar
- 2 teaspoons cornstarch (cornflour)
- 2 teaspoons sweet paprika
- 2 teaspoons hot paprika
- 2 teaspoons ground cumin
- ½ teaspoon salt
- ½ teaspoon black pepper

Spanish chips

- 10½ ounces (300 g) thick-cut potato chips (crisps)
- 10 manzanilla or Gordal olives, pitted and sliced into ¼-inch (5-mm) thick rounds
- 6 Spanish long peppers (*piparras*) or banana peppers, sliced into ¼-inch (5-mm) thick rounds
- 1 (8-oz/230-g) jar assorted pickled vegetables, such as carrots, onions, and gherkin pickles, chopped

method

salsa Espinaler

In a small saucepan, whisk together the vinegar and cornstarch (cornflour). Bring to a boil, then reduce the heat to medium. Simmer for 2–3 minutes and whisk, until the mixture has thickened slightly. Add the spices.

Using an immersion blender, blend everything together (the starch can make it lumpy). Strain, then let cool.

Spanish chips

Arrange the potato chips (crisps) on a serving platter. Drizzle over the salsa. Top with the olives, peppers, and pickled vegetables. Be sure to take a bite of everything with each chip.

Seed and Broccoli Tostada

(30')

In New York, I led a large team at Cosme, one of the city's most popular restaurants at the time, founded by Enrique Olvera. Learning about Mexican culture and leading a diverse team in such an intense city was a crash course in cooking, leadership—and survival.

During this time, I fell in love with tostadas. I love how they can be used as "a spoon" for saucy dishes or as the dish itself, the corn flavor stays prominent no matter what the toppings are. I recommend using organic nixtamalized corn tostadas because they have the authentic taste and heritage of Mesoamerican civilizations.

The seed butter works well here—its water content is low, so it won't make the tostadas soggy. It provides a super-rich layer to the dish.

---

serves 6

seed butter
½ cup (70 g) pumpkin seeds
½ cup (85 g) flaxseeds
⅓ cup (70 g) chia seeds
¼ cup (30 g) hemp seeds
¼ teaspoon salt
½ cup (120 ml) sunflower oil

grilled broccoli
sunflower oil, for frying
1 large broccoli, coarsely grated
1 teaspoon pumpkin seeds
1 teaspoon sunflower seeds
1 teaspoon flaxseeds
1 teaspoon hemp seeds
1 teaspoon chia seeds
¼ teaspoon black pepper
pinch of salt
pinch of chili powder
1 small bunch cilantro (coriander)
1 lime

to serve
6 tostadas or puffed rice crackers
seeds of 1 pomegranate

method

seed butter
Preheat the oven to 350°F (180°C/Gas Mark 4).

Spread the seeds on a baking sheet and toast for 5–10 minutes, until shiny from the released oils. If the heat in your oven is uneven, stir the seeds halfway through toasting. Set aside to cool for 10 minutes.

Place the seeds in a blender, add the salt and sunflower oil, and blend until a smooth paste forms.

grilled broccoli
Heat a drizzle of sunflower oil in a large skillet over medium-high heat. Add the broccoli and sauté until deep brown. Add the seeds and fry for 1 minute until they start to sputter. Season with the pepper, salt, and chili powder. Remove the pan from the heat. Stir in the cilantro (coriander) and a squeeze of lime juice.

to serve
Place the tostadas (or puffed rice crackers) on a serving plate. Top with the seed butter, broccoli, and seeds. Finish with pomegranate seeds and an extra squeeze of lime juice. Serve immediately.

Okra and Asparagus Tempura with Mint-Yogurt Dip

This yogurt sauce was popular at DAR, so we added it as a dip for tasting-menu snacks at KLE. Okra is widely used in Morocco but not so common in Spain, and it's the opposite with asparagus. I like how they retain their juiciness after frying and their intense flavors. It reminds me of a mild mint chutney. Feel free to improvise with other vegetables.

serves 6

mint-yogurt dip

1 cup (220 g) soy or coconut yogurt
¼ cup (15 g) mint leaves, coarsely chopped
½ cup (15 g) cilantro (coriander), coarsely chopped
1½ tablespoons lemon juice
1 tablespoon extra-virgin olive oil
¼ teaspoon salt

okra and asparagus tempura

12 okra
6 asparagus
sunflower oil, for frying
1¼ cups (150 g) all-purpose (plain) flour, plus extra for dusting
½ cup (70 g) cornstarch (cornflour)
½ teaspoon baking powder
¼ teaspoon salt, plus extra to finish
1¼ cups (300 ml) sparkling water

method

mint-yogurt dip

Combine all the ingredients in a blender and blend until smooth.

okra and asparagus tempura

Using a paring knife, gently scrape away the small hairs of the okra pods and trim the stems. Make a small incision down the length of each so steam can escape.

If the asparagus is thick, blanch it in boiling water for 1–2 minutes, then immediately transfer to ice water to stop the cooking. Pat dry with paper towel. Cut each asparagus spear into 3 pieces.

Pour the sunflower oil into a deep saucepan to about 3 inches (7.5 cm) deep. Heat over medium heat to 350°F (180°C).

Meanwhile, prepare the batter. In a bowl, combine the flour, cornstarch (cornflour), baking powder, and salt. Gradually whisk in the sparkling water until the batter is smooth.

Once the oil is ready, toss the okra and asparagus in flour, shaking off any excess. Dip them into the tempura batter, then carefully lower into the hot oil. Deep-fry for 2 minutes, or until the batter is crispy and very light golden. Transfer the vegetables to a paper towel–lined plate to drain excess oil. Season with a little salt.

Serve immediately with the mint-yogurt dip.

Feta-Style Terrine in Kataifi with Maple Drizzle

From my visits to Greece, Egypt, Turkey, and the most eastern part of the Mediterranean, I brought back a love for crunchy golden pastries such as filo (phyllo) and kataifi. A feta-style terrine is wrapped in kataifi threads, baked until super crunchy, and then served drenched in maple syrup and a seed mix. You could also go traditional and use sesame seeds. Crushed almonds would work as well. The combination of salty, sweet, nutty, and acidity creates the perfect bite and takes me back in time to my visits to the Greek islands.

---

serves 6

maple drizzle

- 1 cup (250 ml) maple syrup
- 1 tablespoon sesame seeds, toasted
- 1 tablespoon poppy seeds, toasted
- 1 teaspoon sunflower seeds, toasted

feta-style terrine

- 1 clove garlic, sliced
- ½ cup (125 g) refined coconut oil, melted
- 1 pound (500 g) firm tofu, room temperature, chopped
- ⅓ cup (75 ml) apple cider vinegar
- ¼ cup (15 g) nutritional yeast
- 1 tablespoon salt

assembly

- 1 (1-pound/450-g) package kataifi pastry
- 3½ tablespoons margarine, melted

method

maple drizzle

Mix the maple syrup and toasted seeds in a small bowl.

feta-style terrine

For the "feta," blanch the garlic in boiling water for a few seconds. Drain, then put the garlic into a blender. Add the remaining ingredients and blend until smooth. Pour into a 6 × 5-inch (15 × 12-cm) dish lined with parchment (baking) paper. Refrigerate for at least 2 hours so it's easier to portion.

assembly

Preheat the oven to 375°F (190°C/Gas Mark 5).

Once the cheese has cooled, cut it into 6 equal rectangles, 1 inch (2.5 cm) thick. Wrap each slice of cheese in kataifi pastry. Brush all over with the melted margarine.

Place the packages on a baking sheet lined with parchment (baking) paper and bake for 15–20 minutes, until golden brown.

Serve warm with the maple seed mixture generously drizzled overtop.

Mushroom Bao Buns with Harissa Mayo

This recipe is intended to be a link between the sandwiches found in Morocco's medinas and the bao buns found on the streets of China. Both give me the same satisfaction but use a very different combination of ingredients.

The inspiration for these buns also comes from the freshness of Vietnamese salad rolls and the fluffiness of *min pao* in Peru. The spices—reminiscent of Moroccan street food—in the chermoula marinade are intense, but the pickled veggies bring freshness and a crunchy bite.

Dulse flakes are dried red seaweed with a mild, savory flavor that adds natural saltiness and depth without overpowering a dish. They are commonly sold in health food stores or well-stocked supermarkets.

---

serves 6

steamed buns

- 2 cups (240 g) all-purpose (plain) flour
- 1 tablespoon sugar
- 1 tablespoon active dry yeast
- 1½ teaspoons baking powder
- 1 tablespoon margarine, melted
- ½ teaspoon salt
- sunflower oil, for brushing

pickled vegetables

- 1 carrot, finely julienned
- ½ daikon, finely julienned
- 1 cup (100 g) soybean sprouts
- 2 tablespoons rice vinegar

mushrooms

- Chermoula Marinade (page 263)
- 1 sheet nori, toasted
- 1 teaspoon dulse flakes
- ¼ cup (60 ml) vegetable stock
- juice of ½ lemon
- pinch of salt, plus extra to finish
- 7 ounces (200 g) oyster mushrooms
- ½ cup (60 g) all-purpose (plain) flour
- sunflower oil, for frying

assembly

- Harissa Mayo (page 254)
- Kimchi Togarashi (page 258)
- 6 mint leaves, finely sliced

method

steamed buns

In the bowl of a stand mixer fitted with the dough hook, combine all the ingredients except the salt. Pour in ⅔ cup (150 ml) water. Mix for 2 minutes. Add the salt and mix for another 10 minutes. Cover with a damp kitchen towel and set aside to rise for 1 hour, or until doubled in size.

On a lightly floured surface, roll the dough ¼ inch (5 mm) thick. Use a 3½-inch (9-cm) cookie cutter to cut out 6 circles.

Brush the tops of the circles with oil to help prevent them from sticking together. Fold the circles in half. Gently roll them a little thinner, being careful not to apply too much pressure—you don't want the insides to stick together. Place them on individually cut parchment (baking) papers and arrange on a baking sheet or in a steaming basket with space in between. Proof (prove) for 30 minutes.

When the buns have risen, steam them for 10–12 minutes, until fluffy.

pickled vegetables

Meanwhile, mix all the ingredients in a bowl.

mushrooms

Pour the sunflower oil into a deep saucepan to about 4 inches (10 cm) deep. Heat over medium heat to 350°F (180°C).

Meanwhile, blend the chermoula marinade, toasted nori, dulse, stock, and salt until smooth. Mix 5–6 tablespoons of the marinade with the mushrooms in a large bowl. Let marinate for 10 minutes, then toss the mushrooms in the flour to coat well.

Gently lower the mushrooms into the hot oil in batches and deep-fry until golden and crispy. Transfer to a sheet lined with paper towel to absorb excess oil. Sprinkle with salt.

assembly

Gently open the buns and spread the harissa mayo. Fill with the fried mushrooms, pickled vegetables, and a generous sprinkling of kimchi togarashi. Finish with another drizzle of the mayo, and the chopped mint leaves.

Paella Temaki

I love rice in all its forms—sushi, risotto, mochi, paella, arancini, pudding, all of them. I also love *temaki* bars, where you sit at the counter in front of the sushi chef and they hand you freshly made hand rolls, the rice still warm and the nori crispy. Here, Valencia-style rice is rolled like temaki in a nori sheet; since traditional Valencian paella is usually cooked with seafood, the nori echoes that character by bringing a subtle taste of the ocean.

---

makes 12 temaki

paella

- ⅓ cup (75 ml) extra-virgin olive oil
- 2½ ounces (70 g) sun-dried tomatoes in oil
- 1 onion, finely chopped
- 1 clove garlic, crushed
- 1 teaspoon toasted nori powder
- 1 teaspoon salt
- 1 teaspoon black pepper
- pinch of sweet smoked Spanish pimentón (*pimentón dulce*)
- 4 strands saffron
- 1 bay leaf
- 2 sprigs thyme, finely chopped
- ½ sprig rosemary, leaves only, finely chopped
- 1 cup (200 g) Bomba rice
- 2⅔ cups (630 ml) vegetable stock

to finish

- 3 sheets nori
- Dulse Mayo (page 255) or Wasabi Mayo (page 254)

method

paella

In a small blender, blend the olive oil with the sun-dried tomatoes until you have a coarse paste.

In a large nonstick skillet, add the sun-dried tomato paste, chopped onions and garlic and roast until softened and starting to color. Add the nori powder, spices, and herbs. Stir in the rice and toast for 1 minute. Pour in the stock and stir well. Cook, undisturbed, over low heat for 20 minutes, or until dry and al dente. Remove from the heat and let cool a little.

assembly

Meanwhile, cut each nori sheet into 4 squares and lightly toast them in a pan.

Once the rice is cool enough to handle, place a spoonful of rice on each nori square and roll into cones. Serve the temaki topped with your choice of mayonnaise.

Salads

Salads have never been a side dish in my world. My mother used to eat salad for breakfast—unusual, but it taught me early that a salad can be a full, satisfying meal. That memory still guides me. In summer, I want fresh, crunchy, juicy vegetables; in winter, I lean toward bitter greens, nuts, grains, and anything roasted. Plants change with the seasons, and salads are the easiest way to taste this. I can't think of a more diverse dish to consume on a daily basis without it feeling repetitive.

Working on this chapter reminded me how many directions a salad can take. Sometimes it's as simple as the Spanish Bar Tomato Salad (page 122), where ripe tomatoes and onions do most of the talking. And on colder days, I turn to something with more depth, such as the Crunchy Frisée with Piquillo Peppers and Bean Cream (page 130), where bitterness, sweetness, and creaminess balance each other perfectly. With the help of good *sazón* (page 15) and freshly harvested produce at its peak, a salad can become one of the most exciting and reliable dishes you can make.

Spanish Bar Tomato Salad

I order this salad every time I see it on a tapas bar menu. We serve it for brunch at DAR, and it is the absolute bestseller. The restaurant team also loves ordering it during their break. When tomatoes are in season, they need very little to shine—one of the few natural sources of umami, they are deeply savory and refreshingly cooling in the warm summer months.

The Spanish, just like Italians, are especially proud of their tomato-growing skills, no matter the variety and the specifics of each region. Since tomatoes arrived from South America in the sixteenth century, they have become a part of the Iberian peninsula's identity and an irreplaceable ingredient. Just like rice or corn in some areas of the world, tomatoes are a staple in Spanish homes.

---

serves 4

vinaigrette
½ cup (120 ml) extra-virgin olive oil
¼ cup (60 ml) red wine vinegar
½ teaspoon salt
½ teaspoon black pepper

salad
4 large ripe heirloom tomatoes, cut into bite-size wedges
1 handful cherry tomatoes
2 Tropea or red onions, thinly sliced
5 Spanish long peppers (*piparras*), sliced
10 Arbequina olives
pinch of smoked flaky salt

method

vinaigrette
Whisk the ingredients together in a bowl.

salad
In a bowl, toss the tomatoes and onions with most of the vinaigrette. (Reserve a little to drizzle over the salad before serving.)

Transfer the dressed tomatoes and onions to a serving bowl. Top with the peppers and olives. Drizzle over the remaining vinaigrette and finish with smoked flaky salt.

Watermelon Tomato Salad

The dish was inspired by a particularly hot and humid summer day in Bangkok. After spending the morning walking in the shade of the buildings, we spotted a cute place for lunch. Once inside, cooled by a glass of cold Thai tea, we ordered the most refreshing-sounding dishes on the menu—one of them a watermelon salad.

That first bite—icy, crisp, and full of juice—cut through the heat instantly. When I returned to Switzerland, it happened to be the time our farmers were harvesting melons, including watermelons, so I decided to create a tribute to that salad, which felt like such a gift to us on that day in Bangkok.

This version is different than the original, but it keeps its crisp, refreshing essence. In winter, when watermelons aren't available in Switzerland, we use apples instead.

---

serves 4

watermelon leche de tigre

1½ tablespoons rice
2⅔ cups (400 g) watermelon chunks
juice of 3 limes
1 stalk lemongrass, chopped
1 dried chile, such as guajillo or morilla, stemmed and seeded
1 sheet nori, toasted
3 tablespoons soy sauce or coco aminos
¼ teaspoon salt

salad

4 tomatoes, cut into 1½-inch (4-cm) chunks
1 watermelon, peeled, seeded, and cut into 1½-inch (4-cm) chunks
1 daikon, peeled and cut into 1½-inch (4-cm) chunks

assembly

extra-virgin olive oil, for frying
2 cloves garlic, thinly sliced
1 scallion (spring onion), finely sliced
1 red chile, finely sliced
1 small bunch mint, chopped
1 small bunch cilantro (coriander), chopped
1 handful peanuts, halved and toasted
1 handful store-bought fried onions

method

watermelon leche de tigre

In a skillet, toast the dry rice over medium heat, stirring often, until deep brown but not burned. Set aside to cool for a few minutes. Transfer to a spice grinder and process to a fine powder.

In a blender, process the rice powder and remaining ingredients for 2–3 minutes, until well combined. Refrigerate overnight to develop the flavor.

salad

The next day, in a large bowl, mix together the tomatoes, watermelon, and daikon. Give the leche de tigre a stir, then pour overtop the salad.

assembly

Heat the olive oil in a skillet over medium heat. Add the garlic and fry for 4 minutes, or until golden and crispy. Transfer the crispy garlic to a paper towel–lined plate to drain.

Combine the fried garlic, scallion (spring onion), chile, and herbs in a small bowl.

Transfer the salad to a serving platter and top with the herb mixture. Sprinkle the peanuts and fried onions overtop to finish.

Cucumber, Melon, and "Feta" Salad

This fresh, crisp salad is a great addition to a barbecue. You'll need to use a sweet, ripe melon, and high-quality produce is paramount. If you're pinched for time, you can replace the marinade here with vegan ponzu.

serves 4

marinated cucumber

1 cup (25 g) assorted dried mushrooms
1 cup (250 ml) soy sauce
1 cup (250 ml) lemon juice (about 6 lemons)
1 cup packed (200 g) brown sugar
1 ounce (30 g) kombu
1 large cucumber, unpeeled, quartered lengthwise, and cut into 1-inch (2.5-cm) chunks

salad

1 cantaloupe melon, peeled, seeded, and cut into 1-inch (2.5-cm) chunks
3 shiso leaves, thinly sliced, plus extra for garnish
pinch of salt
extra-virgin olive oil, for drizzling
½ cup (70 g) sesame seeds, toasted
½ cup (54 g) pecans, crushed and toasted
3 tablespoons crumbled Feta-Style Cheese (page 263)
2 tablespoons Apple Honey (page 265)

method

marinated cucumber

Combine all the ingredients except the cucumber in a saucepan and heat over medium-high heat until the sugar has dissolved. Set aside for at least 30 minutes to infuse. Strain the marinade.

Submerge the cucumbers in the marinade and refrigerate overnight.

salad

Remove the cucumbers from the marinade and put them into a large bowl. Add the melon and shiso. Season with the salt and drizzle of olive oil. Toss to mix.

Transfer the salad to a serving platter. Sprinkle with the sesame seeds, pecans, and "feta." Drizzle with the apple honey. Garnish with more shiso leaves.

Raspberry and Beet Salad

Here, a signature salad of Restaurant DAR has been adapted for the home kitchen. The sweetness and acidity of raspberries pairs wonderfully with the earthiness of beets, and the beans create a vibrant combination that gets an extra kick from wasabi.

serves 4

½ cup (120 ml) balsamic vinegar
1 cooked beet (beetroot), peeled and coarsely grated
½ red onion, finely chopped
1½ cups (230 g) drained, canned black beans
1⅔ cups (200 g) raspberries, cut in half
⅔ cup (100 g) corn kernels
¼ teaspoon salt
extra-virgin olive oil, for drizzling
micro basil leaves, for garnish
Wasabi Mayo (page 254)

method

Boil the balsamic vinegar in a small saucepan over high heat until reduced by half. Set aside to cool.

In a large bowl, combine the beet (beetroot), onion, beans, half the raspberries (reserve the nicest ones for garnishing), and corn. Add the salt and a drizzle of olive oil.

Transfer the salad to a serving plate. Using a squeeze bottle, drizzle wasabi mayo overtop. Drizzle over the balsamic reduction following the same pattern. Decorate with the remaining raspberries and basil leaves.

Crunchy Frisée with Piquillo Peppers and Bean Cream

Bitter leafy greens are healthy, delicious and the gourmet version of lettuce. Some people struggle with the bitterness, so I've offset it here with sweet peppers and onions and earthy bean cream.

Leafy greens often lose their crispness during transportation or when handled. To bring them back to their prime, I submerge the raw greens in ice water for 10 minutes before assembling and serving the salad.

---

serves 4

caramelized shallots
sunflower oil, for drizzling
3–4 shallots, thinly sliced
pinch of salt

bean cream
1 (14-oz/400-g) can cannellini beans
4 sprigs thyme
¼ teaspoon ground fennel seeds
¼ cup (60 ml) white wine
1 tablespoon extra-virgin olive oil
2 cloves garlic, crushed
salt
zest and juice of 1 lemon
vegetable stock, for cooking (optional)
black pepper

sherry vinaigrette
½ cup (120 ml) extra-virgin olive oil
¼ cup (60 ml) sherry vinegar
1 tablespoon raw sugar
1 teaspoon smoked paprika
1 teaspoon salt
½ teaspoon black pepper

assembly
2 heads frisée (curly endive), torn into bite-size pieces
4 piquillo peppers, thinly sliced
Croutons (page 41)

method

caramelized shallots
Heat the sunflower oil in a skillet over medium-low heat. Add the shallots and salt and sauté for 1 hour, or until the shallots are softened and caramelized. You can cover the pan with a lid to quicken the process, but good things take time.

bean cream
In a nonstick skillet, combine the beans with their liquid, the thyme, and ground fennel. Cook over medium heat until the liquid has evaporated.

Add the wine and cook for another 5 minutes, or until the mixture has thickened. Add the olive oil, garlic, and a pinch of salt. Fry for 5 minutes, or until the beans have developed a light crust. Stir in the lemon zest and 1 tablespoon lemon juice. Transfer the mixture to a blender and blend into a chunky cream. If needed, add a little vegetable stock to thin out. Season with salt and pepper.

sherry vinaigrette
Blend all the ingredients with ½ cup (120 ml) water in a blender until smooth.

assembly
In a large bowl, toss the frisée (curly endive) with the vinaigrette. Spread the bean cream on a large shallow platter. Arrange the greens overtop. Top with the caramelized shallots, peppers, and croutons.

Crisp Cabbage Salad with Cumin Dressing

30'

A few years ago, three of us traveled to the Maldives to share the work we do at KLE. During the trip, we carved out time to eat and gather ideas—essential to the job. A well-trained palate demands deliberate tasting and eating out. Honestly, it could be worse.

One dinner delivered a mind-blowing Japanese cabbage salad with sesame dressing. It stuck with us so strongly that we created a Moroccan-inspired version for DAR.

I choose to use white and red cabbages because they have very tight coils and sturdy leafage, so it's easier to slice very thin and it stays crunchy after being marinated.

---

serves 4

cumin dressing

1 clove garlic
½ red chile, seeded
juice of 1½ lemons
1 cup (250 g) Vegan Aioli (page 254)
¼ cup (40 g) pine nuts
2 tablespoons nutritional yeast
1 tablespoon ground cumin
1 tablespoon tarragon vinegar
1 tablespoon maple syrup
1 tablespoon soy sauce
¼ teaspoon salt

cabbage salad

sunflower oil, for frying
4 corn tortillas, very thinly sliced
salt
3 tomatillos, diced
1 white (or green) cabbage, shredded with a mandoline
1 red cabbage, shredded with a mandoline
1 avocado
1 scallion (spring onion), thinly sliced
9 ounces (250 g) mesclun salad
1 handful store-bought fried onions
black pepper
8 shiso leaves

method

cumin dressing

Combine all the ingredients in a blender and blend until smooth.

cabbage salad

Pour the sunflower oil into a deep skillet to about 1 inch (2.5 cm) deep. Heat over medium heat to 350°F (180°C). Carefully add the tortilla strips and deep-fry for 10 minutes, or until golden and crunchy. Using a slotted spoon, transfer the tortilla crisps to a paper towel–lined plate to drain. Season with a little salt.

In a large bowl, combine the tomatillos, cabbages, avocado, scallion (spring onion), and mesclun. Add half the tortilla crisps and the fried onions. Add the cumin dressing and toss to mix well. Season with salt and pepper.

Transfer the salad to a serving platter. Top with the shiso leaves. Pit (stone) avocado, then slice and arrange over the salad along with the remaining tortilla crisps. Serve immediately.

Noodles with Peanut Salsa and Cucumber Salad

30'

The way different cultures use peanuts fascinates me. It's clear that in some cultures, peanuts are treated as a legume; in others, including in North Africa, peanuts are grouped with almonds and other nuts. I learned to work with peanuts in Thailand and Mexico, where they are used in sauces, desserts, meat rubs, moles, and much more. This dish draws a connecting line from Thailand to Mexico via Japan.

serves 2

cucumbers

6 Persian cucumbers
2½ tablespoons rice vinegar
1 tablespoon pumpkin seed oil
2 teaspoons soy sauce
1 teaspoon Vegan Aioli without the garlic (page 254)
1 teaspoon sugar
pinch of salt

noodles

3½ ounces (100 g) rice flakes
⅓ cup (80 g) chunky peanut butter
1 tablespoon sunflower oil
4 cloves confit garlic, finely chopped
½ can chipotle peppers, finely chopped
½ cup (70 g) sunflower seeds, chopped
juice of 1 lime
1 handful peanuts, toasted

method

cucumbers

Slice the cucumbers into thin rounds with a sharp knife or a mandoline (be sure to use the guard). Salt generously and place in a colander to drain.

Meanwhile, combine all the remaining ingredients. Blend them together using an immersion blender.

Rinse the cucumbers to remove the salt and pat dry with paper towels. Put the cucumbers into a bowl with the vinaigrette, stir gently, and set aside.

noodles

Bring a pot of water to boil. Add the rice flakes, cover with a lid, and turn off the heat. Cook for 8 minutes (or according to the package directions). Drain, reserving ⅓ cup (75 ml) of the cooking water, and rinse under cold water. Set aside.

In a small bowl, loosen the peanut butter with the reserved cooking water. Place a wok or skillet over medium-high heat and heat the sunflower oil. Add the confit garlic, chipotle peppers, and sunflower seeds and cook for 1 minute, or until the seeds start to pop. Add the peanut butter and noodles and stir-fry for 2 minutes. Squeeze the lime juice over everything.

assembly

Serve the noodles in a bowl, topped with the cucumber salad, toasted peanuts, and another squeeze of lime juice.

Potato Salad

Whenever I'm in a tavern in Spain or Japan, I order potato salad. I also love the versions in Poland, Bulgaria, and Ukraine, plus the ones in the UK and Germany! It seems that every kitchen has its own secret ingredients and ratios.

This recipe is for the potato salad we serve at our wine bar, COR. It's a Spanish potato salad with the best influences from other places. I love to eat this salad between two slices of soft Shokupan (page 68).

serves 4–6

potato salad

- 2¼ pounds (1 kg) starchy potatoes, cut into chunks
- 2 carrots, finely diced
- 7 ounces (200 g) semi-firm smoked tofu, very finely diced
- ½ teaspoon kala namak black salt
- 2 pickles (gherkins), very finely diced
- ½ Fuji or Gala apple, into ½-inch (1-cm) cubes
- 1 cup (250 g) Japanese-Style Mayo (page 254)

toppings

- 4 Spanish long peppers (*piparras*), sliced into rings
- 1 cooked beet (beetroot), peeled and diced
- 1 handful Spanish corn nuts (*kikos*)
- Spanish breadsticks (*picos*)
- 1 small bunch chives, finely chopped

method

potato salad

Put the potatoes in a saucepan with 1 tablespoon of salt and cover with water. Bring to a boil, then simmer for 30 minutes, or until a paring knife easily slides through the center.
Drain the potatoes, then set aside for 10 minutes.

Cook the carrots in salted boiling water for 15 minutes, or until they are softened but still have a little bite. Drain and let cool.

In a bowl, mix the smoked tofu with the black salt.

Once the potatoes have cooled a little, mash half of them with a fork in a large bowl. Add the remaining potatoes, carrots, salted tofu, pickles (gherkins), apple, and mayonnaise. Mix well. Season with a little salt.

toppings

Top the salad with the pepper rings, beet (beetroot), corn nuts, a few breadsticks, and a sprinkle of chopped chives.

Refrigerate any leftovers to enjoy throughout the week—I find that this salad tastes better once the flavors have had a chance to meld.

Grilled Salad

Zaalouk is a Moroccan salad made with grilled eggplants (aubergines) and tomatoes. At KLE, we usually serve it as part of the salad appetizers, but in this recipe we make a cream out of it. This is the most complex salad in this chapter, and it was one of the first dishes that established KLE's identity. It demands more time and care than some of the other recipes, but it rewards the effort.

---

serves 4

zaalouk cream

2 eggplants (aubergines)
1 green bell pepper
2 tablespoons extra-virgin olive oil
3 tomatoes, diced
2 cloves garlic, minced
1 small bunch parsley, finely chopped
1 tablespoon sweet paprika
2 teaspoons ground cumin
pinch of black pepper
½ teaspoon salt
1 lemon

caper dressing

¾ cup (100 g) cashew nuts, soaked overnight
4 cloves garlic
1 cup (200 g) capers
3 tablespoons soy sauce
2 tablespoons aged red miso paste
1 tablespoon Dijon mustard
1 tablespoon lemon juice
1 tablespoon extra-virgin olive oil
½ tablespoon apple cider vinegar
1 teaspoon Tabasco sauce
¼ teaspoon salt

nut-mesan

½ cup (50 g) ground almonds
2 teaspoons nutritional yeast
½ teaspoon onion powder
½ teaspoon garlic powder
pinch of sweet paprika
pinch of salt

vinaigrette

4 tablespoons extra-virgin olive oil
3 tablespoons sherry vinegar
1 teaspoon salt
¼ teaspoon black pepper

to serve

4 heads baby gem lettuce, quartered lengthwise
sunflower oil, for frying
extra-virgin olive oil, for drizzling
1 handful toasted flaked almonds
grated horseradish, for sprinkling
1 sprig dill
1 sprig tarragon
seasonal edible flowers, for garnish

method

zaalouk cream

Preheat the oven to 400°F (200°C/Gas Mark 6).

Using a paring knife, pierce the skin of the eggplants (aubergines) all over. Roast the eggplants and bell pepper for 30 minutes, until charred. Transfer to a bowl and cover with plastic wrap (clingfilm) to trap the steam. Set aside to cool.

Heat the olive oil in a large skillet over medium heat. Add the tomatoes, garlic, parsley, and spices. Season with salt and sauté for 5 minutes, or until the tomatoes are softened. Peel the eggplants. Peel and seed the bell pepper. Coarsely chop both, then add to the pan. Cook for 20 minutes, or until the juices have evaporated. Cool slightly. Add a squeeze of lemon juice, then use an immersion blender to blend until smooth.

caper dressing

Drain the cashews, then rinse them under cold running water. In a blender, combine the cashews with the remaining ingredients and 2 tablespoons water. Blend for 4 minutes, until smooth and creamy.

nut-mesan

In a blender, blend all the ingredients into a powder.

vinaigrette

Whisk all the ingredients and 4 tablespoons water together.

to serve

Reserve half of the lettuce. Drizzle sunflower oil on the cut side of the other half. Pan-fry over high heat until charred.

Drizzle the zaalouk cream and caper dressing on a serving dish. Arrange the raw and grilled lettuce on top, and dress with the vinaigrette. Finish with the toasted almonds, nut-mesan, horseradish, herbs, and flowers.

Soups

In Spain, *platos de cuchara* refer to soothing, comforting dishes you eat with a spoon. It's food that carries love, belonging, and nostalgia in every bite. So it may be no surprise that the recipes in this chapter are the ones I cook most often at home. I've always been a sensitive dreamer who romanticizes food and the stories attached to it, and soups have a special way of transporting me, whether it's back to my childhood or toward a new idea. A single spoonful can set an entire journey into motion.

As the seasons change, so do the soups I crave. In colder months, I reach for warm and aromatic bowls such as Spiced Carrot and Pumpkin Soup (page 149), which wraps me in comfort. When the heat arrives, Silky Melon Gazpacho (page 142) brings that cooling sharpness I love. Even a little spiciness makes the outside air feel cooler. Each of these soups is simple, honest, and carry the spirit of platos de cuchara in its own way.

Silky Melon Gazpacho

My mother-in-law, Teresa, taught me the proper way to make gazpacho. Teresa is from Andalusia, where gazpacho reigns, and—as we say in Morocco—"her hands are blessed" (page 13). Everything she cooks tastes heavenly.

It isn't exact measurements or specific ingredients that make a great gazpacho, but the balance of layers—so that each spoonful is bright and refreshing yet deeply satisfying. This version is an unconventional take on that lesson. For the best results, choose a sweet, ripe Christmas melon and chill it before using. Known in Spain as *Piel de Sapo* (meaning "toad skin"), this muskmelon has thick, mottled green rind, pale green to ivory flesh, and a gentle, mellow sweetness and honeydew-like texture. It's often harvested in late fall and lasts well into December (hence the nickname).

serves 4

- ⅓ cup (20 g) crushed corn tortilla chips
- ½ cup (120 ml) extra-virgin olive oil
- 2 tablespoons sherry vinegar
- 1 ripe Christmas melon (about 3 pounds 5 ounces/1.5 kg), peeled, seeded, and chopped
- ½ green bell pepper, seeded, deveined, and chopped
- ½ cucumber, peeled (reserve the peel) and coarsely chopped
- 1 clove garlic
- 1 teaspoon salt
- ice cubes

to serve

- extra-virgin olive oil, for drizzling
- 1 handful corn tortilla chips, broken up
- cucumber skin, thinly sliced
- 1 handful mint leaves, thinly sliced

method

In a bowl, combine the crushed tortilla chips, olive oil, and vinegar.

In a blender, blend all the remaining ingredients except the ice until smooth. Add ice cubes if the soup is too thick. Pass the soup through a fine-mesh strainer (sieve) if you'd like a smoother gazpacho. Refrigerate until chilled.

Serve the chilled gazpacho in shallow bowls. Drizzle with olive oil. Garnish with broken tortilla chips, cucumber skins, and mint.

Beet Ceviche with Hearts of Palm

Beet (beetroot) grows in a wide variety of climates. At Restaurant KLE, we pair it with spices that offset its earthiness, creating more assertive flavor profiles.

The *leche de tigre* in this dish is made with aromatics, while the marinated heart of palm is standing in for what would be a slice of fish in a traditional ceviche. The ceviches I had tasted in Europe and the United States had animal products in them. In contrast, vegetable ceviches I had in Peru showed a far broader range of ingredients, and it opened my eyes to a world of possibility.

---

serves 6

hearts of palm

8 hearts of palm or pickled asparagus
4 sheets nori

beet (beetroot) sauce

3 stems cilantro (coriander), chopped
1 stalk lemongrass, chopped
½ red onion, sliced
1 cup (120 g) black currant berries
¼ cup (60 ml) black currant juice
¼ cup (60 ml) beet (beetroot) juice
generous ⅓ cup (90 ml) lemon juice (2–3 lemons)
3 tablespoons tamarind paste
1 tablespoon yellow curry paste
½ tablespoon maple syrup
1 teaspoon salt
1 teaspoon chopped turmeric

to serve

10 French Breakfast radishes, thinly sliced
1 scallion (spring onion), thinly sliced
1 handful Spanish corn nuts (*kikos*)
flaky salt
extra-virgin olive oil, for drizzling

method

hearts of palm

Wrap the hearts of palm (or pickled asparagus) in a nori sheet, cutting the excess nori. You can use some water to make sure the nori sticks to the palm. Set aside.

beet (beetroot) sauce

Blend all the ingredients in a blender for 2 minutes, or until smooth. Set aside for 30 minutes to infuse. Strain through a fine-mesh strainer (sieve).

to serve

Cut the nori bundles into ½-inch (1-cm) pieces. Place them in the center of wide, shallow bowls. Top with alternating layers of radishes, scallion (spring onion), and corn nuts. Sprinkle with flaky salt and drizzle with olive oil. Pour the beet (beetroot) sauce around the hearts of palm at the table.

Almond Soup with Grilled Artichokes

(GF) (30′)

Ajo blanco is a traditional cold soup from Andalusia with roots tracing back to the Al-Ándalus period. Historically, it was a humble peasant dish consisting of almonds, garlic, bread, and olive oil, and it was adapted during and after the Spanish Civil War, when ingredients were scarce.

I keep this version gluten-free with the omission of bread and add nutmeg for warmth.

---

serves 4

sunflower oil, for frying
2 small onions (250 g), chopped
3 cloves garlic, minced
1½ teaspoons salt
¼ teaspoon black pepper
1 cup (150 g) raw almonds
¼ nutmeg, grated
4½ cups (about 1 liter) plant-based light (single) cream
3 marinated artichokes, quartered, to serve
extra-virgin olive oil, for drizzling
toasted flaked almonds, for sprinkling

method

Heat the sunflower oil in a saucepan over low heat. Add the onions, garlic, salt, and pepper, and cook gently for 10 minutes, or until the onions are softened. The key is to avoid any browning, to make sure the soup is light and pale.

Add the almonds, nutmeg, and cream. Pour in 1 cup (250 ml) of water and stir well. Cover with a lid and bring to a simmer. Cook for 10 minutes to soften the almonds. Transfer the soup to a blender and blend for 5 minutes, or until smooth. Adjust the consistency and set aside. Heat sunflower oil in a nonstick skillet over high heat. Add the artichokes and sear on all sides until golden.

Serve the ajo blanco in bowls. Top each with 3 slices of the artichokes, a drizzle of olive oil, and the toasted flaked almonds.

Spiced Carrot and Pumpkin Soup

When the days begin to shorten and summer turns to fall, this is my go-to soup for comforting my summer inner child. The sweetness of the pumpkin and the combination of Moroccan spices calm and soothe me. When pumpkin is not in season, sweet potato is a reliable substitute.

---

serves 4

⅓ cup (75 ml) extra-virgin olive oil, plus extra to serve
1 tablespoon brown sugar
2 teaspoons ground ginger
2 teaspoons ground turmeric
3–4 shallots, coarsely chopped
2 large carrots, coarsely chopped
½ pumpkin (10½ oz/300 g), peeled, seeded and coarsely chopped
2 teaspoons salt
4½ cups (about 1 liter) vegetable stock
4 strands saffron
store-bought fried onions, for sprinkling

method

Heat the olive oil in a large saucepan over medium heat. Add the sugar, ginger, and turmeric and toast slightly until fragrant and the sugar has dissolved.

Stir in the shallots, carrots, pumpkin, and salt. Cook for 20 minutes, or until the vegetables start to brown. Pour in the stock and add the saffron. Cover with a lid and simmer over medium heat for 30 minutes, or until the vegetables are softened.

Using an immersion blender, blend until thin and creamy.

Serve hot with a drizzle of olive oil and a sprinkle of fried onions.

Grandma's Soup

This soup is perfect for those chilly days when all you want to do is curl up on the sofa and indulge in a bowl of comfort. My husband's grandma used to make the most delicious soup. His mother learned it from her, and now we also make it at home. Marc is in charge of cooking the vegetable stock base, and I oversee the add-ons, such as barley. It's a popular source of nutrition in the Alps, which has a taste that I love. Sometimes, I finish it with slices of creamy avocado, crunchy fried tortillas, and a squeeze of lime juice.

serves 4

- 6 sprigs thyme
- 1 sprig basil
- 1 sprig sage
- ¼ cup (60 ml) sunflower oil
- 1 teaspoon black pepper, plus extra to season
- 1 tablespoon sweet paprika
- 3 onions, chopped
- 10 cloves garlic
- ½ large (about 14 oz/400 g) celery root (celeriac), cut into ½-inch (1-cm) chunks
- 3 tablespoons nutritional yeast
- 2 teaspoons salt, plus extra to season
- 7 ounces (200 g) oyster mushrooms, shredded, or textured soy protein
- ½ cup (100 g) pearl barley
- 1 lemon
- finely chopped parsley, for garnish

method

Using kitchen string, tie the herb sprigs together to make a bouquet garni.

Put the sunflower oil into a large saucepan. Add the black pepper and paprika and fry for 30 seconds. Add the onions, garlic, celery root (celeriac), nutritional yeast, salt, and bouquet garni. Cook for 5 minutes, stirring continuously. Pour in 8½ cups (2 liters) water. Cover with a lid and simmer over medium-low heat for 30 minutes, or until the vegetables are softened.

In a lightly greased skillet, pan-fry the mushrooms (or textured soy protein) with a pinch of salt and pepper over medium-high heat for 7 minutes, or until browned.

Discard the herb bouquet. Transfer the soup to a blender and blend until smooth. Return the soup to the pan. Add the barley and simmer for 15 minutes. Add the carrots and simmer for another 10 minutes, or until the barley and carrots are cooked through.

Top with the fried mushrooms and a squeeze of lemon juice. Garnish with parsley. Serve immediately.

Sharing Vegetables

Sharing food from the center of the table is a daily occurrence in Morocco. It prevents anyone from disappearing with a plate of food and eating alone in front of a screen! The servings are generous, so each person can eat at their own pace. The rule is simple: Eat from the section in front of you unless someone offers you a taste from their side. This ritual keeps us present.

Plant-based cooking fits naturally into this style of eating, and techniques that build depth are perfect for these shared platters. High-heat roasting concentrates sweetness in vegetables such as carrots and squash. Slow braising transforms cabbage and fennel into something tender with layered aromatics. Acid—preserved lemon, vinegar, citrus—keeps dishes bright even when rich. You'll see these techniques and more featured in many of the recipes in this chapter. For example, Roasted Chermoula Eggplant (page 169) relies on spices blooming in oil; Crispy Cabbage with Tartar Sauce (page 165) shows how texture becomes the star when frying is done well. Each dish is composed to hold its own while contributing to a shared table.

Moroccan Bread Salad

Moroccan bread salad, or *terda*, is akin to *fattoush*, where bread not only gets a second life but becomes the best part of the dish. Here, stale bread anchors a fragrant Moroccan stew built from tomatoes, legumes, spices, and plenty of herbs. What began as a way to avoid food waste has become a home-kitchen staple.

The charm is its simplicity: everyday ingredients, slow-cooked together, turning what might have been thrown out into something deeply comforting and full of flavor.

serves 4

1 cup (180 g) dried fava (broad) beans
1 cup (200 g) brown lentils
3 tablespoons fenugreek seeds
1 tablespoon extra-virgin olive oil
1 tablespoon ras el hanout
1 teaspoon ground turmeric
½ teaspoon ground ginger
3 onions, finely chopped
2 cloves garlic, minced
6 tomatoes, grated
1 red bell pepper, diced
1 bunch parsley, finely chopped
1 bunch cilantro (coriander), finely chopped
salt and black pepper
1 loaf stale bread

method

Combine the fava (broad) beans, lentils, and fenugreek seeds in a large bowl. Cover with cold water, then soak overnight.

Heat the olive oil in a large saucepan over medium heat. Add the ras el hanout, turmeric, and ginger, and cook for 3 minutes, or until fragrant.

Add the onions and garlic and sauté for 5 minutes, or until the onions are softened. Add the tomatoes and red pepper and cook for 2–3 minutes to soften. Drain the bean mixture and add to the pan. Pour in 8½ cups (2 liters) water. Add half the parsley and cilantro (coriander). Reduce the heat to low, cover, and simmer for 1 hour. Season with salt and pepper. Preheat the oven to 350°F (180°C/Gas Mark 4).

Cut the bread into large chunks and spread on a parchment (baking) paper-lined baking sheet. Toast in the oven for 5–10 minutes,until crunchy.

Transfer the bread to a serving bowl and scoop the stew overtop. Garnish with the remaining parsley and cilantro.

White Asparagus with Japanese Mayonnaise and Chives

This dish signals the start of spring across Spain, with a version appearing on bar and tavern menus for a few short weeks each year.

White asparagus is grown buried in soil to prevent sun exposure, which keeps it pale, tender, and gently sweet. Here, it is gently cooked in a lightly sweetened, salted liquid inspired by the brine used for jarred asparagus—something I relied on often as a student. White asparagus is more fibrous than green asparagus and needs to be peeled.

serves 4

white asparagus

16 white asparagus

asparagus cooking liquid

¾ cup (150 g) sugar
2 tablespoons salt

assembly

1 quantity Japanese-Style Mayo (page 254)
1 bunch chives, thinly sliced (see Note)
extra-virgin olive oil, for drizzling
1 lemon
pinch of flaky salt

method

white asparagus

Peel the white asparagus to remove the thick fibers. The flesh should feel smooth and even.

asparagus cooking liquid

Combine the sugar, salt, and 6½ cups (1.5 liters) water in a large saucepan and bring to a boil. Stir until the salt and sugar have dissolved. Add the asparagus and boil for 4 minutes, or until the spears are tender but still have some bite.

Prepare a bowl of ice water and place it next to the pot. Using a slotted spoon, transfer the asparagus to the ice bath to stop the cooking process.

assembly

Dry the asparagus with a kitchen towel and arrange on one side of a serving plate. Put a quenelle of mayo next to the asparagus and top it with the chives. Finish with a drizzle of olive oil, a squeeze of lemon juice, and a sprinkling of flaky salt.

Chef's Note: To slice a bundle of fresh chives as finely as you can, use a sharp knife to trim the ragged ends in one clean cut (save the scraps for stocks or sauces). Keep the bundle tight as you slide the blade back and forth in even strokes instead of pressing down, to keep the cuts clean. Practice with a small bunch, working up to bigger bunches as you perfect the technique.

Tender Leeks with Miso Mayo

In Catalonia, we have a vegetable similar to leeks called *calçots*. Sweet and tender, we char them over a fire, then peel them and eat the steaming flesh. They are milder than leeks and onions, but they are also difficult to find outside of the municipality of Valls. This recipe uses leeks to yield equally tender results.

---

serves 3–4

3–4 large leeks
sunflower oil, for brushing and frying
4 sprigs thyme
2 sprigs rosemary
2 sprigs sage
1 clove garlic, crushed
3 tablespoons extra-virgin olive oil
1 teaspoon salt
½ teaspoon black pepper
1 (14-oz/400-g) can white beans, liquid drained and reserved
6 French Breakfast radishes, quartered
1 tablespoon Miso Mayo (page 255)
1 tablespoon Kimchi Togarashi (page 258) or chopped kimchi

method

Preheat a grill pan over high heat.

Preheat the oven to 375°F (190°C/Gas Mark 5). Brush the leeks generously with sunflower oil. Put them in the hot pan and grill for 10 minutes, or until the outer layers are charred on all sides. Transfer to a baking dish, and add the herbs, garlic, olive oil, salt, and pepper. Cover with a lid or aluminum foil and bake for 30–45 minutes, until the leeks are tender.

Meanwhile, heat 1 tablespoon of sunflower oil in a nonstick skillet over medium heat. Add the beans and fry for 7 minutes, or until lightly browned. Add the reserved liquid and the radishes. Simmer for 5 minutes. Whisk in the mayonnaise.

Peel away and discard the outer layers of the leeks. Arrange the leeks on a serving platter. Spoon the bean sauce overtop. Finish with the kimchi togarashi (or chopped kimchi).

Roasted Carrots with Labneh and Kikos

I could devour this DAR signature dish any day of the week. We spent a lot of time developing this dish because we wanted to bring something fresh and sour to our main courses. Once we cracked the labneh technique, the carrot marinade followed as a natural contrast. It's a well-rounded and approachable combination—perfect for cooking at home.

Kikos are a popular Spanish toasted corn nuts served in bars and movie theaters or enjoyed at home.

---

serves 4

carrot marinade
2 bunches parsley
2 cloves garlic
2 tablespoons ground cumin
1½ tablespoons sweet paprika
1 tablespoon ground turmeric
2 teaspoons ground ginger
2 teaspoons salt
1 teaspoon black pepper
⅓ cup (75 ml) extra-virgin olive oil
¼ cup (60 ml) vegetable stock
2 tablespoons maple syrup
1½ tablespoons soy sauce
juice of 1 lemon

caramelized carrots
1 tablespoon sunflower oil
6 large heirloom carrots (2¼ pounds/1 kg), cut into 4-inch (10-cm) batons
vegetable stock, for cooking (optional)

mojo dressing
2 cloves garlic, minced
1 red pepperoncino or serrano chile, seeded and finely diced
1 small bunch mint, finely chopped
1 small bunch dill, finely chopped
juice of 1 lemon
2 tablespoons extra-virgin olive oil
pinch of salt

assembly
1½ cups (350 g) Labneh (page 262)
2 tablespoons Spanish corn nuts (*kikos*)
grated horseradish (optional)

method

carrot marinade
Place all the dry ingredients in a blender. Then, add the wet ingredients, and blend until smooth.

caramelized carrots
Heat the sunflower oil in a large skillet over medium-high heat. Add the carrots and pan-fry for 10 minutes, or until nicely browned all over.

Pour in the carrot marinade to deglaze. Reduce the heat to medium. Cover with a lid and braise for 5–10 minutes, until the carrots are softened. Check them every couple of minutes, adding a splash or two of vegetable stock, if needed, so that the carrots are nicely glazed.

mojo dressing
Meanwhile, combine all the dressing ingredients in a bowl. Mix well to combine.

assembly
Spread the labneh on a serving plate. Arrange the caramelized carrots in the center and drizzle over the cooking juices. Drizzle with the mojo dressing and finish with the corn nuts. Top with grated horseradish, if you like.

Zucchini alla Scapece with Pistachio Tahini

A few years ago, I traveled through Southern Italy, exploring traditional restaurants and hidden gems across Puglia, Bari, the Amalfi Coast, and Sicily. When dining out, I often order the sides—dishes that tend to reflect what regular guests return for. This is how I discovered *scapece.*

It's a technique for deep-frying seasonal vegetables to crunchy perfection, then soaking them in a sweet-and-sour liquid that will awaken the palate. Vegetables *alla scapece* are a staple in many of those places I visited.

At KLE, we worked on a version to use for a pasta dish, but you can use it as the perfect side to add an exciting new dimension to main dishes.

---

serves 4

scapece marinade
- 1 cup packed (200 g) brown sugar
- 1 cup (250 ml) white vinegar
- 2 cloves garlic, thinly sliced
- 1 bunch mint

zucchini (courgette)
- 4 zucchini (courgette), halved lengthwise
- salt
- sunflower oil, for frying

pistachio tahini sauce
- 3–4 green tomatoes or tomatillos
- 1½ cups (250 g) shelled pistachios
- ½ cup (120 g) tahini
- 1 teaspoon salt
- ¼ teaspoon ground cumin
- juice of 1 lemon
- 4 ice cubes

assembly
- 2 tablespoons shelled pistachios, toasted and finely chopped
- 1 sprig mint

method

scapece marinade
Combine the sugar and vinegar in a saucepan and warm over medium heat until the sugar has dissolved. Add the garlic and mint. Let cool, then refrigerate overnight to infuse. Strain.

zucchini (courgette)
Using a paring knife, score a crisscross pattern into the flesh of the zucchini (courgette). Sprinkle with salt, then lay the zucchini cut side down on paper towels. This will soak up some of the liquid drawn out by the salt.

Pour the sunflower oil into a deep fryer or deep saucepan, about 2 inches (5 cm) deep. Heat over medium heat to 350°F (180°C). Carefully lower the zucchini into the hot oil and fry for 2 minutes on each side, or until golden brown. Work in batches to avoid overcrowding. Using tongs, transfer the zucchini to a paper towel-lined plate to drain. Repeat with the remaining zucchini.

Place the zucchini in a dish, cut side down, and cover with the scapece marinade.

pistachio tahini sauce
Meanwhile, bring a saucepan of water to a boil. Carefully lower in the tomatoes (or tomatillos) and pistachios and blanch for 1 minute. Drain.

Put the tomatoes, pistachios, and remaining ingredients into a blender and blend until smooth.

assembly
Spread the pistachio tahini sauce on a platter. Arrange the zucchini on top. Drizzle with a little scapece marinade. Top with the toasted pistachios and mint sprig.

Crispy Cabbage with Tartar Sauce

30'

This dish brings together tender, braised cabbage and a crisp beer batter, finished with a sharp, herbaceous tartar sauce. My British colleague and friend, Emily, put on her English hat and developed a batter she could stand behind.

The cabbage is first gently braised to soften and deepen its flavour, then coated and fried until golden. The result is a contrast of textures, with the tartar sauce adding brightness and acidity to balance the richness.

---

serves 4

braised cabbage

3½ tablespoons margarine
1 large hispi cabbage, cut into 4 wedges
2 cloves garlic, minced
½ cup (120 ml) white wine
½ cup (120 ml) vegetable stock
1 tablespoon white wine vinegar
1 teaspoon Apple Honey (page 265) or maple syrup
pinch of salt

beer batter

½ cup (60 g) cornstarch (cornflour)
½ cup + 1 tablespoon (75 g) all-purpose (plain) flour
1 teaspoon baking powder
¼ teaspoon salt
⅔ cup (150 ml) lager

mayonnaise base

zest and juice of 1 lemon
4 tablespoons aquafaba
1 tablespoon tarragon vinegar
1 teaspoon Dijon mustard
1 teaspoon nutritional yeast
½ teaspoon salt
¼ teaspoon black pepper
pinch of kala namak black salt
1 cup (250 ml) sunflower oil

tartar sauce

1 tablespoon capers, chopped
1 pickle (gherkin), finely chopped
2 teaspoons pickle (gherkin) liquid
1 small bunch dill, finely chopped
1 small bunch parsley, finely chopped
1 small bunch chives, finely chopped
1 shallot, finely chopped
salt and black pepper

assembly

sunflower oil, for deep-frying

method

braised cabbage

Melt the margarine in a skillet over medium-high heat. Add the cabbage and brown on all sides. Reduce the heat to medium-low. Add the garlic and cook for 1 minute.

Deglaze with the wine and bring to a boil. Add the stock, vinegar, and honey (or maple syrup). Cover with a lid and simmer for 15 minutes, or until the cabbage is softened. Transfer the cabbage to a paper towel–lined plate to cool.

beer batter

Meanwhile, in a bowl, combine all the ingredients except the lager and mix well. Slowly whisk in the lager until the batter is smooth. Let rest for 20 minutes.

mayonnaise base

In a medium bowl and using an immersion blender, blend together all the ingredients except the oil. Gradually pour in the sunflower oil, blending until the mixture is thickened.

tartar sauce

Stir the tartar sauce ingredients into the mayonnaise base. Season with salt and pepper.

assembly

Pour the sunflower oil into a deep fryer or deep saucepan, about 4 inches (10 cm) deep. Heat over medium heat to 350°F (180°C).

Once the cabbage has cooled, dust each wedge with a little flour, shaking off any excess. Dip in the beer batter, making sure the wedges are well coated. Carefully drop into the hot oil and fry until golden brown. Using a slotted spoon, transfer to a baking sheet lined with paper towel to drain. Sprinkle with salt.

Serve the cabbage wedges on a plate with a bowl of the mayo-tartar sauce on the side for dipping.

Grilled Spiced Cauliflower with Couscous

The Amazigh—my ancestors—are the indigenous people of North Africa. (The term translates to "free people" or "noble people.") Slow cooking over firepits has long sustained them and makes sense for a nomadic life.

This spice rub nods to my people and southern tagine; the cauliflower, being a sponge, drinks in all that flavor.

---

serves 4

grilled spiced cauliflower

4 onions, thinly sliced
sunflower oil, for frying
pinch of salt
1 large cauliflower, cut into large florets
2 tablespoons Amazigh Spice Blend (page 259)
1 tablespoon extra-virgin olive oil

couscous

2 cups (360 g) couscous
3 tablespoons extra-virgin olive oil
3⅓ cups (800 ml) vegetable stock
1 teaspoon salt, plus extra to taste
½ teaspoon black pepper, plus extra to taste
1 small bunch mint, finely chopped
1 small bunch cilantro (coriander), finely chopped
1 small bunch parsley, finely chopped

assembly

1 tablespoon sunflower oil
1 small bunch mint, finely chopped
1 small bunch parsley, finely chopped
1 small bunch cilantro (coriander), finely chopped
2 tablespoons harissa paste

method

grilled spiced cauliflower

Heat the sunflower oil in a skillet over medium-low heat. Add the onions and salt and gently sauté for 1 hour, or until caramelized. Set aside.

Steam the cauliflower for 5 minutes. Let cool slightly, then mix in a bowl with the Amazigh spice blend and olive oil.

couscous

Put the couscous into a large bowl and massage the olive oil into it, making sure all the grains are coated.

In a saucepan, bring the vegetable stock to a boil. Season with the salt and pepper. Pour the stock over the couscous. Mix well and cover immediately with a lid to trap the steam. Set aside for 20 minutes to steam.

Stir in the chopped herbs. Season with salt and pepper.

assembly

Heat the sunflower oil in a nonstick skillet over high heat. Add the cauliflower and fry for 10 minutes, or until brown.

Transfer the couscous to a serving plate. Top with the cauliflower and caramelized onions. Sprinkle with the chopped herbs. Serve with the harissa paste on the side.

Roasted Chermoula Eggplant

In Morocco, we talk about *chermoula* like Italians talk about tomato sauce—chermoula goes with everything, and everyone loves it. Whether it's in raw salads, with baked vegetables, or over tagines, chermoula is the queen of marinades and the ultimate representation of the Moroccan palate. It's a balanced canvas of garlic, spices, and lemon juice, and its many variations include parsley, cilantro (coriander), or chiles.

I often cook eggplants (aubergines) over a charcoal grill because the smoky notes complement it so well, but feel free to cook as you like.

---

serves 4

roasted eggplants

2 eggplants (aubergines)
1 tablespoon salt
5 cloves garlic, finely chopped
½ cup (120 ml) lemon juice
3 tablespoons extra-virgin olive oil
2 tablespoons sweet paprika
1 tablespoon smoked paprika
1 tablespoon ground cumin
1 teaspoon black pepper

vinaigrette

¼ cup (60 ml) extra-virgin olive oil
¼ cup (60 ml) white balsamic vinegar
½ teaspoon salt

pearl (giant) couscous salad

½ cup (80 g) pearl (giant) couscous
extra-virgin olive oil, for drizzling
1 red onion, finely chopped
1 green serrano pepper, finely chopped
1 pear, unpeeled, cored, and finely chopped
½ preserved lemon, peel only
1 bunch cilantro (coriander), finely chopped
1 bunch parsley, finely chopped
1 small bunch mint, finely chopped

assembly

arugula (rocket), for topping

method

roasted eggplants

Preheat the oven to 400°F (200°C/Gas Mark 6). Line a baking sheet with parchment (baking) paper.

Halve the eggplants (aubergines) lengthwise. Using a sharp knife, cut a crisscross pattern into the flesh. Salt generously, place cut side down in a colander, and drain in the sink for 10 minutes.

Meanwhile, in a bowl, make the chermoula by combining the garlic, lemon juice, olive oil, sweet and smoked paprikas, cumin, and pepper.

Blot the eggplants with paper towel to remove the salt. Drench the eggplants with chermoula, reserving a few tablespoons. Bake for 30–40 minutes, until soft and the top is bubbling and golden brown. Brush with the reserved chermoula, then bake for another 15–20 minutes, until soft and the top is bubbling and golden brown.

vinaigrette

Combine all the ingredients in a small bowl. Add 2 tablespoons water and whisk together.

pearl (giant) couscous salad

Boil the couscous for 8–10 minutes, until al dente. Drain, then stir in a drizzle of olive oil. Let cool.

Combine the couscous and remaining ingredients in a large bowl. Add the vinaigrette and toss to mix.

assembly

Place the eggplants in the center of a serving plate. Top with the pearl couscous salad and arugula (rocket).

Fried Eggplant with Spicy Tomato Sauce over Arroz Rojo

Growing up, my mom used to make breaded and fried eggplant (aubergine) cutlets *(escalopes)* all the time—and I loved it. It's the perfect way to spotlight vegetables. Her version included chopped parsley and minced garlic in the breading, so feel free to add those here if you like.

This dish also works well using giant oyster mushrooms or celery root (celeriac) as a substitution for the eggplants.

serves 4

spicy tomato sauce

- 3 tablespoons extra-virgin olive oil
- 1–2 red onions, finely chopped
- 2 cloves garlic, finely chopped
- 1 teaspoon salt, plus extra to taste
- 1½ tablespoons tomato paste (puree)
- 1 tablespoon harissa paste
- ¼ teaspoon black pepper, plus extra to taste
- ¼ teaspoon ground cumin
- 2–3 tomatoes, chopped
- 2 cups (475 ml) vegetable stock

eggplants

- 4 eggplants (aubergines)

arroz rojo

- 2 tablespoons extra-virgin olive oil
- 1 onion, finely diced
- 1 carrot, finely diced
- 1 clove garlic, minced
- 1 teaspoon salt
- 2 tomatoes, finely diced
- 1 cup (200 g) white rice
- 2 cups (475 ml) vegetable stock
- ½ cup (60 g) frozen peas

assembly

- 1¼ cups (150 g) all-purpose (plain) flour
- 2 cups (300 g) panko bread crumbs
- sunflower or vegetable oil, for frying
- pinch of salt

method

spicy tomato sauce

Heat the olive oil in a skillet over medium heat. Add the onions, garlic, and salt. Sauté for 5 minutes, until the onions are softened. Add the tomato paste (puree), harissa, pepper, and cumin. Cook for a minute, until fragrant.

Add the tomatoes and stock. Simmer for 45 minutes–1½ hours, until the sauce has thickened. Season with salt and pepper.

eggplants

Preheat the oven to 375°F (190°C/Gas Mark 5).

Using a paring knife, pierce the skin of the eggplants (aubergines) all over. Bake for 30 minutes, until soft to the touch. Transfer the eggplants to a container and cover with an airtight lid. Set aside for 15 minutes to cool.

arroz rojo

Heat the oil in a saucepan over medium heat. Add the onion, carrot, garlic, and salt. Sauté for 10 minutes, until lightly colored. Add the tomatoes and cook for 2 minutes.

Stir in the rice and stock, then bring to a boil. Reduce the heat to medium-low and simmer for 10–15 minutes, covered, until the rice is al dente. Add the peas and simmer for 5 minutes.

assembly

Meanwhile, gently peel off the aubergine skins, keeping the flesh attached at the stem end so that the eggplants are intact. Place on a plate and gently flatten with the back of a flat knife.

Place a third of the flour in a shallow bowl. In a second bowl, combine the remaining two-thirds of the flour with 1 cup (250 ml) water and stir until smooth. Place the bread crumbs in a third bowl. Dip an eggplant into the flour, shaking off the excess. Dip it into the batter, making sure it is well coated. Roll it in the panko, pressing it lightly to help the panko stick. Repeat with the remaining eggplants.

Pour the oil into a deep fryer or deep saucepan, about 2 inches (5 cm) deep. Heat over medium heat to 350°F (180°C). Carefully lower the eggplants into the oil and deep-fry each side for 5 minutes, until golden brown and crunchy. Work in batches to avoid overcrowding. Using tongs, transfer the eggplant to a paper towel–lined plate to drain. Season with salt.

Spoon the rice into a serving platter. Arrange the eggplant on a separate plate. Pour over the spicy tomato sauce. Serve the extra sauce in a sharing bowl.

Bakoola

This dish is a true representation of "ugly delicious." My Moroccan aunts would always place it on the table as a mezze to start the meal. It was green, messy, and very unappetizing to me until I reluctantly tried it. And once I tasted it, I had to have more.

Bakoola is a delicious warm salad of robust greens—kale, arugula (rocket), cabbage, Swiss chard, spinach, and broccoli—slowly cooked with spices.

---

serves 4

bakoola
2 tablespoons extra-virgin olive oil
4 cloves garlic, minced
2 teaspoons smoked paprika
2 teaspoons ground cumin
pinch of cayenne pepper
1 pound (500 g) mixed greens, such as Swiss chard, kale, savoy cabbage, finely chopped
1 bunch parsley, finely chopped
1 bunch cilantro (coriander), finely chopped
½ teaspoon salt, plus extra to taste
½ preserved lemon

assembly
1 cup (250 ml) balsamic vinegar
½ cup (75 g) Feta-Style Cheese (page 263)
1 handful pine nuts, toasted
1 sprig dill, picked

method

bakoola
Heat the olive oil in a large skillet over medium heat. Add the garlic and spices and sauté for 30 seconds, or until fragrant. Stir in the mixed greens, parsley, cilantro (coriander), and salt. Cover with a lid and cook for 20 minutes, stirring occasionally, until the leafy greens are softened. Season with salt.

In a small blender, combine the pulp of the preserved lemon and ¼ cup (60 ml) water. Blend until smooth. Add the mixture to the skillet.

assembly
In a small saucepan, simmer the vinegar over high heat until reduced by half. Transfer the bakoola to a shallow serving dish. Crumble the "feta" on top and drizzle with the balsamic reduction. Sprinkle with the pine nuts and dill.

"Okonomiyaki"

I am amazed by cultural connections between countries thousands of miles apart, sometimes with gigantic bodies of water between them. In this case, I share a recipe that brings together a traditional dish from Catalonia, one from Osaka and Hiroshima in Japan, and one from the Swiss Alps.

Okonomiyaki is a Japanese savory pancake served with bonito flakes, scallions (spring onions), and sauces. Pyrenees *trinxat* is made with potatoes, cabbage, and pork. Sometimes it is served mashed, but my favorite version is fried like a pancake until a golden crust forms. *Rosti*, a Swiss dish, is simply crisp, shallow-fried grated potatoes. It's considered farmer food and is usually topped with eggs, bacon, and cheese (the Swiss "holy trinity").

These three dishes have different histories, but they all give me the same feeling—a sense of tradition and pride in making modest ingredients taste amazing.

---

serves 2

2 large potatoes (10½ oz/300 g), peeled
9 ounces (250 g) smoked tofu
4 tablespoons soy sauce
2 tablespoons shiro miso paste
½ teaspoon baking powder
pinch of salt
1 small green (white) cabbage (10½ oz/300 g), thinly sliced with a mandoline
2 scallions (spring onions), finely sliced
2 cloves garlic, minced
sunflower oil, for frying

to serve

¼ cup (60 ml) BBQ sauce (optional)
½ quantity Japanese-Style Mayo (page 254)
⅓ cup (50 g) sesame seeds, toasted
2 sheets nori, toasted and crumbled

method

Using a large box grater, grate the potatoes and tofu. Wrap the potatoes in a kitchen towel and squeeze over a sink to remove the excess water.

In a medium bowl, whisk together the soy sauce, miso, baking powder, and salt.

In a separate bowl, combine the cabbage, tofu, scallions (spring onions), and garlic. Add the miso dressing and toss.

Heat a thin layer of oil in an 8-inch (20-cm) nonstick skillet over medium heat. Place half the vegetable mixture in the middle of the pan and pat it down flat. Reduce the heat to low, cover with a lid, and cook for 15–20 minutes. Carefully transfer the "okonomiyaki" to a plate, then flip it back into the pan to fry the other side. Cover and cook for 20 minutes, or until the edges are crunchy. Repeat for the second okonomiyaki.

Serve on plates, drizzled with the BBQ sauce, if desired, and mayonnaise. Sprinkle with the sesame seeds and nori.

Pineapple, Plantain, and Okra Stew

I couldn't make my mind up between sharing with you an okra tagine, a *sancocho*, or a pineapple rice, so I worked on a dish featuring all the parts I like from each dish. This stew is delicious over steamed rice and, as with almost any stew, it tastes better the next day.

---

serves 6

stew

- 15 okra
- 1 large plantain, peeled and cut into ¼-inch (5-mm) slices
- ½ cup (120 ml) sunflower oil, plus extra for frying
- 2 cinnamon sticks
- 1 stalk lemongrass, cut into thirds
- 2 teaspoons mustard seeds
- 2 teaspoons ground cumin
- 2 onions, finely chopped
- 1¼ teaspoons salt
- 3 pandan leaves, cut into 2-inch (5-cm) slices
- 2 red chiles, finely sliced
- 1 tablespoon ras el hanout
- 8½ cups (2 liters) unsweetened coconut milk
- 1 pineapple, cut into 1-inch (2.5-cm) chunks
- 1 bunch cilantro (coriander), chopped

rice

- 1 cup (200 g) jasmine rice

method

stew

Wash the okra well, then wipe each piece with paper towel to remove the fuzz from the surface.

Cut away the hard tops, then cut each piece of okra into 3 pieces. Pan-fry in a little oil over high heat until golden brown but not soft. Set aside.

Pour frying oil into a skillet, about ½ inch (1 cm) deep. Heat over medium heat to 350°F (180°C). Carefully add the plantain and fry until lightly colored on both sides. Remove the pan from the heat and smash each plantain slice with the back of a spoon. Fry again until evenly golden brown. Set aside.

Heat the sunflower oil in a large saucepan over medium heat. Add the cinnamon sticks, lemongrass, mustard seeds, and cumin and fry for 2–3 minutes, until fragrant. Add the onions and salt and sauté for 7 minutes, or until they are softened. Add the pandan leaves and chiles and cook for 5 minutes, or until everything is golden brown. Add the ras el hanout and stir for 1 minute. Pour in the coconut milk. Bring to a boil and add the fried okra, fried plantain, and pineapple.

Cook over low heat for 20 minutes, or until the stew starts to thicken and the coconut milk splits. Discard the lemongrass and pandan.

rice

Meanwhile, in a saucepan, bring the rice and 1⅓ cups (325 ml) cold water to a boil. Reduce the heat to low and cover. Steam for 12 minutes—do not remove the lid.

assembly

Stir the cilantro (coriander) into the stew. Serve family-style with the rice.

Chef's Note: The lemongrass and pandan should be big enough that you can see them in the stew and remove them before serving.

Comfort

Comfort sits at the center of how I cook and how I remember home. When I make *canelons* (page 199), or when the smell of Mushrooms with Spit-Roast Spices and Potatoes (page 192) fills the kitchen, I'm transported straight back to the places and people who shaped me. These dishes were never meant to be vegan, so recreating them with plants has been a long and deeply personal process. I kept testing until the flavors resonated in my heart as the originals had. Only when a dish could make me feel that old familiarity when I closed my eyes did I know I had achieved it.

What continues to surprise me is how others react when they taste these versions. Friends who grew up with these dishes often fall quiet, then smile, sometimes even becoming a little emotional. They tell me it feels like home to them too.

These recipes show that the feeling we chase in food can be rebuilt with care, patience, and plants. If you cook even one of them, I hope you feel a little of that same warmth rise up in your own kitchen. You may even revisit your own recipes in the same way, with the process stirring a sense of nostalgia and yielding surprising results.

Tamagoyaki "Arroz a la Cubana"

My dad had a signature dish that would always make my brother and me super happy. It was rice with scrambled eggs, with a smiley face drawn in ketchup on top. It was quick and always a safe bet. My mom had her own version, which was closer to *arroz a la cubana*, which is rice with tomato sauce and a fried egg. I loved them both equally.

In Tokyo, I was surprised to find many takes on a similar idea, some echoing my dad's, others closer to my mom's. It felt natural to bring those influences together in this dish.

---

serves 2

ketchup

2¼ pounds (1 kg) ripe cherry tomatoes, cut into quarters
sunflower or vegetable oil, for frying
⅔ cup (130 g) sugar
⅔ cup (150 ml) white vinegar
1 tablespoon garlic powder
1 tablespoon onion powder
1 tablespoon mustard powder
1 tablespoon nutritional yeast
2 teaspoons salt
1 teaspoon tomato paste (puree)
black pepper

rice

1 cup (200 g) sushi rice, rinsed
2 tablespoons rice vinegar
1½ tablespoons sugar
1 teaspoon salt

omelet batter

7 ounces (200 g) silken tofu
½ cup (60 g) mung bean starch
½ cup (120 ml) vegetable stock
1 tablespoon dashi or mushroom oyster sauce
2 tablespoons soy sauce
2 tablespoons raw sugar
1 teaspoon nutritional yeast
½ teaspoon kala namak black salt
¼ teaspoon ground turmeric
pinch of salt

method

ketchup

Heat a drizzle of oil in a large skillet over high heat. Add the tomatoes and fry for 3–5 minutes, until the tomatoes start to color. Add the remaining ingredients. Stir well and then cook for 1 hour, or until the liquid has evaporated.

Using an immersion blender, blend the mixture into a smooth sauce. Store the ketchup in a jar in the refrigerator for up to 1 week.

rice

Combine the rice and 2 cups (500 ml) of water in a saucepan over medium-high heat. Bring to a boil. Reduce the heat to low, then cover with a lid. Cook for 20 minutes, or until the rice is tender and all the water has been absorbed. Remove from the heat and set aside.

omelet batter

In a blender, combine all the ingredients. Let rest for 5–10 minutes.

Heat a 12-inch (30-cm) nonstick skillet over medium heat. Blend the batter again with an immersion blender to incorporate a little air. Spoon a ladleful into the pan so it covers the surface in a thin layer. Cook until the batter has just set, then roll it into a log on one side of the pan and push it to the edge. Add another ladleful of batter to the pan. Once set, roll the first log up in the second layer. Repeat two more times, then remove the rolled omelet from the pan. Cut into thick slices.

assembly

Season the sushi rice with the vinegar, sugar, and salt. Serve the omelet with the rice and a ramekin of ketchup.

Tofu Katsu Sando

I've always loved sandwiches, especially the way they bring together different textures in a single bite. This one leans into that contrast: crisp, golden tofu layered into soft, milky shokupan, with a rich miso mayo and a hint of truffle.

The tofu is marinated for depth, then coated in a light batter and panko for a delicate crunch. Creamy, savory, and just a little indulgent, it elevates a familiar katsu sando into something more refined.

---

serves 4

marinated tofu
- 2 teaspoons sugar
- 2 teaspoons mirin
- 1 teaspoon shiro miso paste
- 1 teaspoon soy sauce
- ¼ teaspoon salt
- ¼ teaspoon kala namak black salt
- 10½ ounces (300 g) semi-firm tofu, sliced into 4 equal pieces

batter
- 1¼ cups (150 g) all-purpose (plain) flour
- 3¾ cups (300 g) panko bread crumbs
- sunflower or vegetable oil, for frying
- salt

assembly
- 8 slices Shokupan (page 68)
- 3½ tablespoons margarine, melted
- Miso Mayo (page 255)
- truffle paste or fresh truffle shavings
- 3½ cups (100 g) baby spinach

method

marinated tofu
Combine all the ingredients except the tofu in a bowl. Mix until smooth.

Place the tofu in a 6-inch (15-cm) square dish. Pour in the marinade and cover. Set aside on the counter for 1–2 hours.

batter
Measure out ¾ cup (90 g) of the flour. Put the remaining flour in a shallow bowl. In a second bowl, whisk together the reserved flour with 1 cup (250 ml) water until smooth. Put the panko in a third bowl.

Pour the oil into a deep saucepan to about 4 inches (10 cm) deep. Heat over medium heat to 350°F (180°C).

Once the tofu is marinated, carefully dip each slice first in the flour, shaking off any excess. Dip into the batter, making sure it is well coated, and finally into the panko, rolling it as you press lightly to help the panko stick.

Fry the tofu katsu in the oil until the panko is golden brown. Transfer to a baking sheet lined with paper towel. Sprinkle lightly with salt.

assembly
Lightly toast the shokupan slices and brush with the melted margarine. Spread a spoonful of miso mayo on a slice of toast. Layer with a generous handful of spinach leaves, laid neatly over each other.

Spread some miso mayo on another slice of toast, followed by a spoonful of the truffle paste (or truffle shavings). Place the fried tofu on top of the spinach. Close the sandwich and cut in half. Serve.

"Pastrami" Sandwich

Working late nights in New York City, I wanted something to eat before heading home after finishing my shift. Corned beef and pastrami sandwiches were available almost everywhere, and I became a fan.

serves 4

"pastrami"
2 tablespoons ground coriander
1 tablespoon sweet paprika
1 tablespoon mustard powder
1 teaspoon black pepper
½ teaspoon salt
½ cup (120 ml) extra-virgin olive oil
28 ounces (800 g) oyster mushrooms

assembly
8 slices Rye Bread (page 67)
hot mustard
Burger Sauce (page 187)
½ cup (70 g) sauerkraut
8 pickles (gherkins), sliced lengthwise

method

"pastrami"
Preheat the oven to 350°F (180°C/Gas Mark 4). Line a baking sheet with parchment (baking) paper.

In a bowl, mix the spices with the olive oil. Stir in the oyster mushrooms, making sure they are well coated. Marinate for 20 minutes.

Shake off any excess marinade and place on the prepared baking sheet. Bake for 15 minutes. Turn the mushrooms over and bake for another 15 minutes, or until they are completely dry on the outside.

assembly
Spread 4 slices of rye bread with hot mustard and 4 with burger sauce. Top with a spoonful of sauerkraut, fried mushrooms, and pickles (gherkins). Close the sandwiches with the sauced slices of rye.

Smash Burger

I discovered smash burgers while living in the United States. It is the opposite concept to the classic juicy, thick, medium-rare burger, so it took some time to settle in Europe, but now they are everywhere. At our cocktail bar, we serve a delicious smash burger, its well-browned patty boasting the characteristic crispy edges.

---

serves 6

caramelized onions

4 tablespoons sunflower oil
5 large onions, finely sliced
pinch of salt

burger patty

¾ cup (100 g) textured soy protein or mince
4 tablespoons chia seeds
4 tablespoons soy sauce
2 tablespoons nutritional yeast
1 tablespoon BBQ sauce
1 tablespoon extra-virgin olive oil
2 teaspoons Sriracha
½ teaspoon smoked paprika
½ teaspoon garlic powder
¼ teaspoon liquid smoke

burger sauce

1 cup (250 g) Vegan Aioli (page 254)
3 tablespoons ketchup
4 teaspoons mustard
4 tablespoons pickle (gherkin) juice
2 teaspoons white vinegar
1 teaspoon smoked paprika
½ teaspoon onion powder
½ teaspoon garlic powder
½ teaspoon salt

assembly

6 potato burger buns (page 188)
6 slices vegan cheese
6 crisp lettuce leaves
1 tomato, sliced

method

caramelized onions

Heat the oil in a saucepan over low heat. Add the onions and salt and cook for 1 hour, or until golden and caramelized.

burger patty

Meanwhile, blend ⅓ cup (40 g) of the soy protein (or mince) with the chia seeds in a spice grinder until you have a fine powder. Put the mixture into a bowl with the remaining soy protein.

Combine the remaining ingredients in a saucepan. Add ⅔ cup (150 ml) water and bring to a boil. Pour the mixture over the soy protein and stir well. Cover the bowl with plastic wrap (clingfilm) and let steam for 20 minutes. Remove the plastic wrap and put the mixture in the refrigerator to cool.

burger sauce

In a bowl, mix together all the ingredients.

assembly

Once the patty mixture has cooled, divide it into 6 equal balls. Flatten each ball between two sheets of parchment (baking) paper. In a nonstick skillet over medium-high heat, fry the patties for 2–4 minutes per side, until golden brown.

Slice and toast the potato buns. Spread both sides generously with the burger sauce.

For each burger, place a lettuce leaf and slice of tomato on the flat side of the bun. Add the patty, a slice of vegan cheese, and a spoonful of the caramelized onions. Finish with the top bun.

KFM Burger

If there's one dish guests remember from KLE or DAR, it's the KFM—KLE Fried Mushrooms. It grew out of my nostalgia for the fried food of the American South, especially the meals I had in Louisiana during my final month living in the United States. Back in the kitchen, I kept testing until I landed on something that truly satisfied that craving.

Here, those mushrooms are reworked into a burger, paired with a soft, slightly sweet bun inspired by the ones I remember. Crisp, saucy, and indulgent, it's a playful take on a fast-food classic.

---

serves 6

burger buns
1 quantity Glazed Sweet Potato Milk Buns dough (page 72)

buttermilk herb mayo
½ cup (120 ml) unsweetened soy milk
1⅔ cups (400 ml) sunflower oil
½ teaspoon salt
zest and juice of ½ lemon
1 bunch dill, finely chopped
1 bunch tarragon, finely chopped
1 bunch chervil, finely chopped

hot sauce
½ cup (120 ml) maple syrup
½ cup (120 ml) Sriracha
scant ½ cup (100 g) margarine

batter
scant 2½ cups (300 g) all-purpose (plain) flour
2 teaspoons garlic powder
2 teaspoons onion powder
1 teaspoon ground turmeric
1 teaspoon salt
¼ cup (60 ml) unsweetened oat milk

fried mushrooms
12 large oyster mushrooms
sunflower or vegetable oil, for frying
pinch of salt

assembly
6 crisp lettuce leaves
3 pickles (gherkins), sliced lengthwise

method

burger buns
Instead of shaping the dough into mini buns, divide it equally into 6 (3½-oz/100-g) balls of dough. Bake according to recipe.

buttermilk herb mayo
Pour the soy milk into a tall pitcher (jug). Slowly drizzle in the sunflower oil, blending continuously with an immersion blender to emulsify. Stir in the salt, lemon zest and juice, and chopped herbs.

hot sauce
Combine the ingredients in a saucepan and heat over medium heat until the margarine has melted. Blend with an immersion blender to emulsify.

batter
In a bowl, mix together all the dry ingredients. Whisk in the oat milk and ⅔ cup (150 ml) water until smooth.

fried mushrooms
Dip each mushroom into the batter, making sure it is well coated, then toss it in the seasoned flour, patting it gently on each side to make sure it sticks.

Pour the oil into a deep saucepan to about 4 inches (10 cm) deep. Heat over medium heat to 350°F (180°C). Carefully add the battered mushrooms and fry for 5 minutes, or until golden and crunchy. Using a slotted spoon, transfer to a bowl. Sprinkle with a pinch of salt, then glaze generously with the hot sauce.

assembly
Slice and toast the burger buns. Spread both sides with the herb mayo. Place a lettuce leaf on each burger bun bottom. Top with 2 fried mushrooms and a few slices of pickles (gherkins). Drizzle over a little more of the mayo and enjoy!

Cachapa-Style Corn Omelet

Corn was an indigenous food in Mesoamerica and pre-Hispanic cultures that merchants introduced it to Japan during the spice trade.

Corn has followed me throughout my career, but I didn't fully appreciate it until I was executive sous chef at Cosme in New York. Many of the chefs were Venezuelan and often cooked staff meals, and the first time I tasted a *cachapa*, it stopped me in my tracks. This pancake-like discovery stole my heart at first bite.

Crispy caramelized edges, a sweet and savory spongy inside—it perfectly encapsulates the flavors of fresh corn and toasted corn flour, making it the perfect blanket for stuffings. So when it came to deciding which corn dish to include in this book, a Venezuelan-style cachapa with Vietnamese stir-fried corn was the clear winner.

Serves 2

cachapa
- 2 cups (280 g) corn
- 1 tablespoon flaxseeds, finely blended
- ¾ cup (100 g) arepa flour (see Note)
- pinch of salt
- ½ cup (120 ml) unsweetened rice or soy milk
- sunflower oil, for frying
- 3½ tablespoons margarine

filling
- sunflower oil, for frying
- 3½ ounces (100 g) Swiss chard, leaves finely chopped and stems finely sliced
- 1⅔ cups (250 g) corn
- ½ teaspoon salt

assembly
- ¼ cup (55 g) salty crunchy peanut butter
- ½ cup (115 g) vegan cream cheese or Labneh (page 262)
- salted peanuts (optional)

method

cachapa

Drain canned corn kernels, if using. If using fresh corn, blanch the kernels in boiling water for a few seconds.

Bloom the flaxseed powder with 3 tablespoons water. Combine the arepa flour, corn, flaxseed mix, and milk in a food processor. Blend into a thick batter.

Heat a drizzle of sunflower oil in an 11-inch (28-cm) nonstick skillet over high heat. Add a medium ladleful of batter to form a thin pancake. Reduce the heat to low and cook for 10 minutes, or until golden brown.

Add a little margarine to the pan, then very carefully flip the cachapa to cook on the other side for another 10 minutes. Repeat the process with the remaining batter.

filling

Heat the oil In a pan over high heat. Add the chard stems and corn and fry until the water from the stems has evaporated and the vegetables are lightly charred. Add the chard leaves and fry for another 2–3 minutes, until the leaves have wilted and any liquid has evaporated. Remove from the heat and season with salt.

assembly

Spread crunchy peanut butter on half of each cachapa. Scoop filling onto the peanut butter, then fold the cachapa over the filling. Serve topped with a dollop of cream cheese (or labneh) and a sprinkling of salted peanuts, if you like. Alternatively, put the filling and capachas in separate bowls in the center of the table and let people assemble their own.

Chef's Note: Arepa flour is a precooked white corn flour, known in Spanish as harina P.A.N, made from maize that has been cooked, dried, and finely ground. It is essential for dishes such as empanadas. It is available from Latin American grocers, well-stocked international supermarkets, and online retailers.

Mushrooms with Spit-Roast Spices and Potatoes

Pollo a l'ast is a classic Sunday family meal that you buy from food trucks or takeout windows across Catalonia, Valencia, and other regions in Spain. It is usually accompanied by soggy french fries saturated in the fatty spit-roast chicken juices. I, and millions of people who grew up on the Mediterranean coast, have memories of family weekends eating *pollo a l'ast* out of aluminum containers.

Here, I use oyster mushrooms instead of chicken. I recommend using fresh Agria potatoes—the younger they are, the less starchy and the crispier they become when fried. I've prepared chunky fries, but for shoestring fries, cut the peeled potatoes into matchsticks. A mandoline with a julienne attachment works best—just be sure to use the guard.

---

serves 4

1 bay leaf
½ nutmeg, grated
2 teaspoons salt
2 teaspoons black pepper
1 teaspoon dried oregano
1 teaspoon dried rosemary
1 teaspoon dried thyme
1 teaspoon ground cumin
1 clove garlic, minced
3 tablespoons extra-virgin olive oil
1 pound (500 g) oyster mushrooms
2¼ pounds (1 kg) young Agria potatoes
vegetable oil, for frying
½ cup (120 ml) vegetable stock

to serve

Vegan Aioli (page 254)
1 lemon, cut into wedges (optional)

method

Process the herbs and spices for the spice blend in a spice grinder. In a bowl, mix the ground spices with the garlic and olive oil.

In a large bowl, generously coat the mushrooms with the spice marinade. Set aside to marinate for 30 minutes.

Meanwhile, peel the potatoes. Cut them into thick batons, about 2 × ½ inch (5 × 1 cm). Place them in a bowl of cold water to remove as much starch as possible.

Drain, then place them on paper towels to dry. Pour the vegetable oil into a deep saucepan, about 4 inches (10 cm) deep. Heat over medium-low heat to 285°F (140°C). Carefully add the batons and deep-fry until they are softened but without any color. Remove with a slotted spoon.

Heat the oil to 350°F (180°C). Return the batons to the oil and deep-fry until golden and crunchy. Transfer the fries to paper towels to absorb the excess oil, then salt generously.

In a skillet over high heat, fry the mushrooms until golden brown. Deglaze the pan with the vegetable stock, then remove from the heat.

Serve your fries topped with the mushrooms and cooking juices. Serve with aioli on the side and a few wedges of lemon, if desired. Enjoy!

Ramp Gnocchi, Sobrasada, and Pine Nuts

Northern Italy is renowned for its gnocchi, and the islands of Palma de Mallorca for its *sobrasada*. Both regions shared a culture for a very long time, and in this dish we bring them back together. Ramps (wild garlic) are available only for a few weeks each spring and super popular in Switzerland. They combine a grassy spring flavor with the pungent and sharp taste of garlic. I always add it to the menus when in season. At home, I like it in a simple pasta dish or stir-fry.

This dish takes a bit of planning, since the gnocchi dough rests overnight, but it's well worth it. You can freeze leftover plain gnocchi on a sheet of parchment (baking) paper, then transfer to an airtight container once frozen solid. You can also freeze the sobrasada separately.

serves 6

sobrasada

- 2 sweet potatoes, unpeeled
- 4 sun-dried tomatoes in oil
- 1½ teaspoons ground cumin
- 1½ teaspoons sweet smoked Spanish pimentón (pimentón dulse)
- ½ teaspoon salt

ramp (wild garlic) gnocchi

- 2¼ pounds (1 kg) starchy potatoes, washed
- 20 ramp (wild garlic) leaves, chopped
- scant ½ cup (100 ml) extra-virgin olive oil
- 1 cup (170 g) fine semolina, plus extra for dusting
- 1 cup (130 g) bread flour
- ¼ nutmeg, grated
- 1 tablespoon salt
- ¼ teaspoon white pepper
- 1 tablespoon sunflower oil

to serve

- ¾ cup (100 g) pine nuts, toasted
- ramp leaves and flowers (optional)
- extra-virgin olive oil, for drizzling

method

sobrasada

Preheat the oven to at 375°F (190°C/Gas Mark 5).

Bake the sweet potatoes in their skins for 45–60 minutes, until soft.

Remove the sweet potatoes from the oven. Once cool enough to handle, peel off the skin. Place the flesh in a blender with the remaining ingredients. Blend to a smooth paste.

ramp (wild garlic) gnocchi

While the sweet potatoes for the sobrasada are baking, steam the starchy potatoes for 30–40 minutes. (Alternatively, boil them until a knife easily slides through the center.) Remove the potatoes from the pot and peel them while still warm. Mash using a potato ricer. Put the mashed potatoes in a baking dish and store uncovered in the refrigerator overnight. This will allow them to dry out a little for fluffier gnocchi.

Prepare a bowl of ice water. Blanch the ramp (wild garlic) leaves in a pot of boiling water for a few seconds. Transfer to the ice bath to stop the cooking process. Remove from the ice bath and squeeze out the excess water. Coarsely chop the leaves, then blend with the olive oil in a small blender to create a paste.

In a large bowl, mix together the semolina, flour, and seasonings. Make a well in the middle and fill it with the potatoes and ramp oil. Gently knead everything into the potato until you have a smooth, non-sticky dough. Form into a large ball and cover with a damp kitchen towel.

Portion the dough into smaller balls and roll them into logs, 1 inch (2.5 cm) in diameter. Cut the gnocchi using a bench scraper and place on a baking sheet dusted with semolina.

Bring a saucepan of salted water to a boil. Cook the gnocchi until they float to the surface. Using a slotted spoon, transfer them to a clean kitchen towel. (Reserve some of the cooking water.)

Heat the sunflower oil in a nonstick skillet over medium-high heat. Add the gnocchi and fry until they have a golden crust. Add a few spoonfuls of the sobrasada and a splash of the gnocchi cooking water to the pan, stirring to coat.

to serve

Serve the gnocchi in bowls, topped with toasted pine nuts and garnished with ramp leaves and flowers. Finish with a drizzle of olive oil.Serve with sobrasada sauce.

Toasted Noodles

This dish is a Catalan take on paella, made with short toasted noodles instead of rice and served with garlicky aioli. Known as *fideuà*, it's a staple along the Mediterranean coast where I grew up.

In this version, fine vermicelli noodles take on deep, oceanic flavor from the broth, while the seasoning *mar i muntanya*, meaning "sea and mountain," brings a balance similar to surf and turf. If you don't have time to make aioli by hand, you can use the quicker version on page 255.

serves 4

seaweed stock

2 sheets kombu (about ¾ oz/20 g)
2 sheets nori
1 bulb fennel, halved
1 bay leaf
1 cup (25 g) mixed dried mushrooms
1 cup (250 ml) dry white wine
1 tablespoon nutritional yeast
1 teaspoon juniper berries

Catalan seasoning *(mar i muntanya)*

1 clove garlic, chopped
pinch of salt
1 teaspoon brown sugar
2 strips orange peel, chopped
3 strands saffron
12 almonds, toasted
10 leaves parsley, chopped
1 tablespoon vegan dark chocolate chips (at least 74%)
3 tablespoons extra-virgin olive oil
juice of 1 orange

traditional aioli

4 cloves garlic
pinch of salt
juice of ½ lemon
extra-virgin olive oil, for drizzling

fideuà

1 tablespoon sunflower oil
1 white onion, finely chopped
½ scallion (spring onion), thinly sliced
2 cloves garlic, crushed
5–6 button mushrooms, finely chopped
1–2 king oyster mushrooms, finely chopped
½ red bell pepper, seeded, deveined, and finely chopped
¾ teaspoon salt
1 tomato, coarsely grated
1½ teaspoons sweet paprika
10 strands saffron, soaked in 1 tablespoon hot water
3 tablespoons extra-virgin olive oil
5½ ounces (150 g) short vermicelli *(fideos)*
½ lemon, for serving

method

seaweed stock

Combine all the ingredients in a large saucepan. Pour in 4½ cups (about 1 liter) water and bring to a boil. Reduce the heat to medium-low, cover, and simmer for 1 hour.

Catalan seasoning *(mar i muntanya)*

Using a mortar and pestle, pound the ingredients, adding them one by one in the order listed. Muddle in the oil and juice.

traditional aioli

Using a mortar and pestle, crush the garlic. Add the salt and juice of half a lemon. Drizzle with olive oil and a few drops of water as you pound the mixture to a creamy consistency.

fideuà

Heat the sunflower oil in a nonstick skillet over medium heat. Add the onion and scallion (spring onion) and sauté for 6 minutes, until tender. Add the garlic and cook for 5 minutes. Add the mushrooms, bell peppers, and salt, and cook for 20 minutes, or until everything has nicely browned. Stir in the tomato, paprika, and soaked saffron, crushing the threads between your fingers to break them up. Cook until the tomato juice has evaporated.

Preheat the oven to 350°F (180°C/Gas Mark 4).

Add the olive oil and vermicelli to the pan and stir for 3 minutes, until the noodles are toasted. Spread the aioli overtop the noodles, if you like.

Strain the seaweed stock through a fine-mesh strainer (sieve). Pour 1⅓ cups (325 ml) into the pan and stir well. Spread out the noodles and cook, untouched, for 5 minutes. Transfer the pan to the oven and cook for another 10 minutes, or until all the liquid has been absorbed and the noodles are golden and slightly crispy on top.

To finish the *fideuà*, drop spoonfuls of the Catalan finishing paste evenly over the entire surface. Squeeze a little lemon juice on top and enjoy!

Roast Cannelloni with Bechamel

December 26 is St. Esteve, a celebratory day in Catalonia, and it's also my mother's birthday. It's common to eat *canelons de rostit amb beixamels*, for St. Esteve—cannelloni with a stuffing made with the leftovers of the Christmas roast. We didn't celebrate Christmas in our house, but I spent a lot of time at my neighbors' home when they did! My mother-in-law makes the best *canelons*. She always made extra to send to my brother when he was studying abroad.

In this recipe, we use cauliflower with all the aromatics of a Christmas roast. If you have time, I encourage you to make fresh pasta (page 264) as we do at the restaurants, but this version is meant to be easy to make at home.

---

serves 6

cauliflower filling

- 2 tablespoons sunflower oil
- 2 red onions, chopped
- 2 carrots, chopped
- ½ leek, white and light green parts only, thinly sliced
- salt
- 1 head cauliflower (9 oz/250 g), coarsely grated
- 2½ cups (250 g) textured soy protein or mince
- ¼ teaspoon ground cumin
- ¼ cup (60 ml) soy sauce
- 1 cup (250 ml) dry white wine
- ¼ teaspoon black pepper, plus extra to taste
- 1 bay leaf
- 1 sprig thyme
- 1 sprig rosemary
- 5 cups (1.2 liters) vegetable stock
- 1 quantity Onion Bechamel (page 264)

cannelloni

- 2 cups (475 ml) plant-based light (single) cream
- 12 sheets lasagna

method

cauliflower filling

Heat the sunflower oil in a saucepan over medium-high heat. Add the onions, carrots, leek, and a pinch of salt. Sauté for 10 minutes, or until tender and golden. Add the cauliflower, soy protein (or mince), and cumin. Increase the heat to high and cook until the vegetables start to brown.

Deglaze the pan with the soy sauce and wine. Add 1 teaspoon salt, the black pepper, and bay leaf. Tie the herb sprigs with kitchen string. Once the wine has evaporated, reduce the heat to low. Pour the stock over the vegetables and simmer for 1 hour, or until all the liquid has evaporated.

Discard the herb bouquet and transfer the mixture in a food processor. Pulse to a coarse consistency. Transfer the mixture to a bowl and stir in 1 cup (280 g) of bechamel. Season with salt and pepper to taste. Set aside.

cannelloni

In a saucepan, heat the cream over medium heat until reduced by half. Remove from the heat. Bring a saucepan of salted water to a boil. Prepare a bowl of ice water and place it next to the pan. Parboil the lasagna sheets for 4 minutes, or until flexible and al dente. Transfer to the ice bath to stop the cooking process. Lay the lasagna noodles between two clean kitchen towels to dry.

Preheat the oven to 350°F (180°C/Gas Mark 4).

Brush a baking dish with olive oil. Scoop a spoonful of the cauliflower mixture on one end of a lasagna noodle. Roll into a log. Repeat with the remaining lasagna noodles and filling. Place them side by side in the baking dish. Cover with the remaining bechamel and reduced cream.

Bake the cannelloni for 15 minutes, or until the surface is bubbling and golden.

Remove from the oven and let cool for a few minutes. Serve family-style.

Coca Catalana

This recipe takes me back to my student dorm two decades ago, to a cramped room full of books and unsorted clothes. On days when we didn't have to study, one of us would cook, and we'd all eat straight from the hot pan.

In Catalonia, instead of pizza, we have *coca de recapte*—a simple flatbread topped with whatever vegetables were on hand. It's humble, adaptable, and deeply tied to place, capturing the flavors of the Mediterranean coast.

This version holds onto those student days, when we gathered around a tiny table or perched on the edge of a bed, enjoying a quick but homemade meal that tasted like love and comfort when we were feeling homesick.

---

serves 6

crust (base) and vegetable layer

2 eggplants (aubergines)
1 red bell pepper
1 package store-bought puff or filo (phyllo) pastry
melted margarine or extra-virgin olive oil, for brushing
flaky salt

topping

3 sun-dried tomatoes in oil, finely chopped
2 cloves garlic, crushed
2 tablespoons Moroccan black olives or Kalamata olives, finely sliced
2 teaspoons capers, chopped
3 tablespoons extra-virgin olive oil
1 lemon

to finish

1 small bunch parsley, finely chopped
Feta-Style Cheese (page 263) (optional)
flaky salt

method

crust (base) and vegetable layer

Preheat the oven to 400°F (200°C/Gas Mark 6). Line a baking sheet with parchment (baking) paper.

Pierce the skin of the eggplants (aubergines) and bell pepper. Bake them for 30 minutes, or until softened. Remove from the oven. Transfer the vegetables to a bowl and cover with plastic wrap (clingfilm) to trap the steam. Set aside to cool.

Once cool, peel the eggplants and bell pepper. Remove the seeds from the pepper. Cut the eggplants and pepper into thick strips and set aside.

Preheat the oven to 400°F (200°C/Gas Mark 6).

Line a baking sheet with parchment (baking) paper and place half of your pastry on top. Brush with water, then place the other half on top. Brush with margarine (or olive oil). Sprinkle generously with flaky salt. Bake the crust for 5–10 minutes, until golden and crunchy.

Remove from the oven and fill with the eggplant and bell pepper. Bake for another 10–15 minutes, until golden brown.

topping

In a bowl, combine the sun-dried tomatoes, garlic, olives, and capers. Add the olive oil and a squeeze of lemon juice.

assembly

Spoon the topping over the base. Garnish with parsley. Crumble soy feta on top, if you like, and sprinkle with flaky salt.

Desserts

At our restaurants, we try to take people back to their childhood memories with our desserts. The team comes from many backgrounds, so we put real care into finding flavors that feel familiar to everyone in some way. I stay away from anything too abstract or overly technical, because it's often the simplicity of that first sweet taste that we remember.

To create decadent plant-based desserts, I use plenty of seasonal fruit for acidity and balance, so that nothing becomes too sweet or too heavy. Spices, flowers, and naturally sweet vegetables, such as pumpkin, sweet potato, or beets help build depth without relying on dairy. Flan con Nata (page 204) shows how silky a custard can be, while Grandma's Cookie Cake (page 226), with its layers of cream and cookies that soften into something familiar, brings nostalgia to the table. The Butternut Squash Cheesecake (page 214) proves how creamy and rich a vegan dessert can be when cashew nuts, miso, and roasted squash work together. These desserts are simple, balanced, and meant to leave you with a lasting sense of comfort at the end of a meal.

Flan con Nata

I used to flip straight to the dessert section of the menu to see if it had *flan con nata*. In my mind, flan was the perfect sweet end to any meal, so I didn't bother tasting other restaurant desserts if flan was on offer.

The other kind of flipping I recall is the one done to get the flan out of the container, when you want to serve it on a plate. At home, we always had artisanal flans in the refrigerator, and I loved to bet with my brother which of us could flip a flan fastest and smoothest onto the dessert plate without making a mess of the caramel.

serves 6

caramel

1 cup (200 g) raw sugar
3 tablespoons lemon juice
3 tablespoons orange juice
½ teaspoon ground cinnamon

flan

1⅔ cups (390 ml) plant-based light (single) cream
½ teaspoon agar agar or vegan gelatin
½ teaspoon cornstarch (cornflour)
½ teaspoon vanilla powder
pinch of ground turmeric
pinch of kala namak black salt
4½ ounces (125 g) vegan white chocolate, finely chopped

assembly

½ cup (120 ml) plant-based heavy (double) cream
1 tablespoon sugar
seasonal berries (optional)

method

caramel

In a small saucepan, combine the sugar with ½ cup (120 ml) water. Heat over medium heat, swirling the pan occasionally without stirring, until the bubbles become thicker and the mixture turns a dark amber. Remove from the heat and carefully stir in the lemon and orange juices and cinnamon. Pour the caramel into 6 flan molds. Place in the freezer until needed.

flan

In a saucepan, whisk together all the ingredients except the white chocolate. Bring to a boil, then reduce the heat to medium. Simmer for 3 minutes, whisking continuously.

Add the chocolate and remove the pan from the heat. Stir until the chocolate has melted. Let cool at room temperature for 20–30 minutes.

Pour the flan mixture slowly into the flan molds on top of the caramel base. Refrigerate for at least 2 hours, until the flan has set.

assembly

Whip the cream and sugar with a hand mixer until stiff.

To serve, warm the flan molds by rubbing them in your hands. Place a plate upside down on top of a mold and, in one quick, smooth motion, flip the flan out onto the plate. Repeat with the remaining flans. Serve topped with the whipped cream and seasonal berries, if you like.

Chocolate Custard with Whipped Cream

Copa de chocolate con nata, a popular Spanish store-bought dessert, was my brother's favorite, so I made it my mission to create a plant-based version that he would approve of. After experimenting with different techniques and ingredients, I found that cornstarch is the component that helps the chocolate set with a soft yet bouncy texture, just like the original.

serves 4

whipped cream

¾ cup (175 ml) plant-based whipping cream
3 tablespoons confectioners' (icing) sugar
1 teaspoon cream of tartar

chocolate custard

3 tablespoons cornstarch (cornflour)
2 cups (500 ml) unsweetened almond milk
5 ounces (150 g) vegan dark chocolate
¾ cup (75 g) raw sugar
¼ cup (60 g) margarine

method

whipped cream

Whip the cream, confectioners' (icing) sugar, and cream of tartar with a hand mixer until the mixture holds its shape. Set aside in the refrigerator.

chocolate custard

In a small bowl, mix the cornstarch (cornflour) with ¼ cup (60 ml) of the milk until smooth. Pour the cornstarch slurry into a saucepan along with the remaining milk and the custard ingredients. Cook over low heat for about 5 minutes, stirring continuously, until the chocolate has melted and the mixture starts to thicken.

Divide the custard between 4 serving coupes or ramekins. Refrigerate for at least 30 minutes to set.

Serve the puddings topped with whipped cream. You could also add a drizzle of salted caramel or seasonal fruit, if you like.

Chai Ice Cream with Rhubarb Compote

When the seasons change and the farmers start bringing us different vegetables, we always go through a process of trial and error in the kitchen. During one rhubarb season, we paired the rhubarb with various tea blends and realized that the fruitiness of red rooibos matches it well.

This dish is aromatic, refreshing, and a perfect way to end a meal, especially because rooibos has no caffeine. (The ice cream contains black tea and we didn't want to overdo it.) The contrast in textures between the fruit compote, the infusion, and the ice cream creates a balanced, refreshing finish.

---

makes 6½ cups (1.5 liters) ice cream

ice cream base

- 4½ cups (about 1 liter) unsweetened oat milk
- ⅔ ounce (20 g) fresh ginger
- 2 black peppercorns
- 2 cardamom pods
- 2 star anise
- 2 cloves
- 1 cinnamon stick
- 1 teaspoon fennel seeds
- 1½ teaspoons black tea
- 1⅓ cups (325 ml) sunflower oil
- ½ cup (100 g) sugar
- 3 tablespoons cornstarch (cornflour)
- 1 tablespoon glucose (see Note)
- pinch of salt

rhubarb compote

- 2 tablespoons sugar
- 1 tablespoon red rooibos tea
- 2 sticks rhubarb (about 5 oz/150 g), finely diced
- ½ cup (120 ml) rhubarb juice

method

ice cream base

In a saucepan, combine the milk, spices, and black tea. Bring to a boil over medium heat, then remove it immediately from the heat. Let infuse for 30 minutes.

Strain the milk through a fine-mesh strainer (sieve) and return to the saucepan. Add the sunflower oil, sugar, cornstarch (cornflour), glucose, and salt. Cook for 5 minutes over medium heat, stirring continuously. Cool it down in an ice bath.

Pour the base into an ice cream maker. Churn for 15–30 minutes, until it reaches soft-serve consistency. Freeze for 2 hours, or until firm.

If you don't have an ice cream maker, place the mixture in a large flat container and freeze until solid. Cut the ice cream into large chunks and pulse in a food processor to a smooth consistency. Transfer to an airtight container and freeze for 1–2 hours, until ready to serve.

rhubarb compote

In a saucepan, combine the sugar, ½ cup (120 ml) water, and the rooibos tea. Heat over medium heat until the sugar has dissolved. Remove from the heat and let infuse for 20 minutes.

Put the rhubarb into a saucepan along with the rhubarb juice. Strain the rooibos tea syrup into the pan. Cook over medium heat for 5 minutes, or until the rhubarb is softened but still holds its shape. Set aside to cool slightly.

Transfer the lukewarm rhubarb compote to serving dishes. Top with the ice cream.

Chef's Note: To prevent the glucose from sticking to your measuring spoon, first dip the spoon in water.

Moroccan Sundae with Rose Water Ice Cream

When I was younger, if my mom was having a difficult day, she would hand me a few coins and ask me to get her a sundae with caramel sauce and toasted peanuts. I'll never forget the way that first spoonful seemed to soften whatever burden she was carrying. It brought her a moment of peace. My mother didn't have an easy start in life, but she fought tirelessly to change her path—and she did. So, if a sundae brought her even a little comfort, I made sure to run as fast as I could to get it.

This dessert is a tribute to the classic sundae, reimagined with North African flavors. Now my mother can have it anytime at DAR, because as long as the restaurant exists, this sundae will always be on the menu. Photo on page 212.

---

serves 6

rose water ice cream

1 cup (250 ml) light (single) plant-based cream
1 cup (250 ml) unsweetened rice milk
3 cardamom pods
1 cinnamon stick
1½ tablespoons cornstarch (cornflour)
½ cup (120 ml) sunflower oil
⅓ cup (75 g) sugar
2 teaspoons glucose
pinch of salt
2 teaspoons rose water

lemon and white chocolate cookie dough

¾ cup (100 g) all-purpose (plain) flour
3½ tablespoons margarine
⅓ cup (75 g) sugar
seeds of 1 vanilla bean
zest of 1 lemon
pinch of salt
2½ tablespoons unsweetened almond milk
3½ ounces (100 g) vegan white chocolate, chopped into small pieces

toffee

⅓ cup (75 g) sugar
1 cup (250 ml) plant-based light (single) cream
1 tablespoon margarine
seeds of 1 vanilla bean
pinch of salt

caramelized nuts

9 ounces (250 g) nuts of your choice
⅓ cup (70 g) sugar
4½ teaspoons margarine

candied cherries

1 pound (500 g) cherries, pitted (stoned)
2 tablespoons jam sugar (aka gelling sugar)

whipped cream

scant ½ cup (100 ml) plant-based heavy (double) cream
2 tablespoons sugar

method

rose water ice cream

In a saucepan, combine the cream, rice milk, cardamom, and cinnamon. Bring to a boil, then immediately remove it from the heat. Let infuse for 1 hour.

Strain the mixture through a fine-mesh strainer (sieve) and return it to the saucepan. Mix the cornstarch (cornflour) with 2 tablespoons of the mixture. Add the slurry to the pan along with the sunflower oil, sugar, glucose, and salt. Cook for 5 minutes over medium heat, whisking continuously. Transfer to an ice bath, then stir in the rose water.

Pour the ice cream base into an ice cream maker. Churn for 15–30 minutes, until it reaches soft-serve consistency. Freeze it for 2 hours, or until firm.

If you don't have an ice cream maker, put the base in a large flat container and freeze until solid. Cut the ice cream into large chunks and pulse in a food processor to a smooth consistency. Transfer to an airtight container and freeze for 1–2 hours, until ready to serve.

lemon and white chocolate cookie dough

Toast the flour in a nonstick skillet, stirring often, until light brown and nutty.

Combine the margarine, sugar, vanilla seeds, lemon zest, and salt in the bowl of a stand mixer fitted with the paddle attachment. Beat on high speed for 5 minutes, until light and fluffy. Reduce the speed, then add the almond milk. Beat in the flour. Mix in the white chocolate. Store the cookie dough in the refrigerator or freezer until ready to serve.

toffee

Simmer the sugar and 3 tablespoons water in a small saucepan over medium-low heat until it turns to a medium amber–colored caramel. Don't stir the mixture or it may crystallize. If needed, use a pastry brush dipped in water to brush down the sides of the pot.

Remove the caramel from the heat and carefully pour in the cream. Whisking vigorously, add the margarine, vanilla seeds, and salt. Return the pan to the stove over medium-low heat and simmer for 15 minutes, or until the color deepens to a medium brown. Let cool at room temperature.

caramelized nuts

Preheat the oven to 350°F (180°C/Gas Mark 4).

Toast the nuts in the oven for 10 minutes, or until golden brown.

Meanwhile, cook the sugar in a saucepan over medium heat until melted and a medium amber. You can swirl the pan to distribute the sugar while it melts but do not stir it or it will crystallize.

Add the warm nuts and margarine to the caramel and stir to coat the nuts. Transfer the nuts onto a baking sheet, using a spatula to spread them out to cool. Stir the nuts every few minutes while they cool to prevent them from sticking together.

candied cherries

Combine the cherries and sugar in a saucepan. Bring to a boil over medium heat and simmer for 2 minutes. Set aside to cool.

whipped cream

Using a hand mixer, whip the cream with the sugar until the mixture holds its shape.

assembly

Serve the ice cream in bowls. Add a handful each of caramelized nuts and candied cherries. Top with a few pieces of cookie dough. Finish with a spoonful of whipped cream and a drizzle of toffee.

Butternut Squash Cheesecake

A good cheesecake is creamy and rich with a slightly tart, umami flavor. For this plant-based version, our team uses miso and nutritional yeast to bring that umami and savoriness.

This dessert can be baked a couple of days ahead, then served with various toppings—from fresh seasonal fruit to jams and compotes, to a simple spoon of sweetened whipped cream.

The cashews need to soak for at least 24 hours, so plan accordingly. The longer the soaking time, the more intense the flavor will be.

---

serves 8–10

cheesecake

½ butternut squash, peeled, seeded, and cut into chunks
2¼ cups (300 g) cashew nuts, soaked in water for 24–48 hours
¼ cup (65 g) shiro miso paste
1 cup (220 g) raw sugar
1 cup (230 g) vegan cream cheese
⅓ cup (50 g) all-purpose (plain) flour
1 tablespoon apple cider vinegar
1 teaspoon vanilla powder
1 teaspoon nutritional yeast
½ teaspoon salt
¼ teaspoon baking powder

crumb crust (base)

1 cup (100 g) rolled (porridge) oats
1¼ cups (150 g) all-purpose (plain) flour
⅓ cup packed (70 g) muscovado sugar or dark brown sugar
1 teaspoon ground cinnamon
½ teaspoon salt
½ cup (120 g) margarine, room temperature

method

cheesecake

Preheat the oven to 350°F (180°C/Gas Mark 4/Gas Mark 4). Line a baking sheet with parchment (baking) paper.

Spread the squash on the baking sheet and cover with aluminum foil. Bake for 30–40 minutes, until completely soft. Remove from the oven and let cool. Keep the oven on.

crumb crust (base)

Meanwhile, line the bottom and sides of a 9-inch (22-cm) cake pan with parchment (baking) paper.

Process all the crumb crust (base) ingredients in a food processor to a crumbly cookie consistency. Press the crumb into the bottom of the prepared cake pan in an even layer. Bake for 15 minutes.

assembly

Increase the oven temperature to 410°F (210°C/Gas Mark 6½). Place a lipped baking sheet in the oven, and fill it with water, ½ inch (1 cm) deep.

Return to the cheesecake. Drain the nuts and rinse under running water. In a food processor, combine the nuts, miso paste, and 1½ cups (300 g) of the cooked pumpkin. Pour in ¼ cup (60 ml) water and process for 5 minutes, or until smooth and yogurt-like in consistency. If needed, add a tablespoon of water to thin the mixture.

In a large bowl, combine the mixture with the remaining cheesecake ingredients. Mix until smooth.

Pour the cheesecake filling into the prebaked crust in the cake pan. Smooth the top with a spatula. Place the cheesecake on the water-filled sheet. Bake for 35–40 minutes, until the center of the cake feels set but soft inside when you press it with your fingertip.

You can serve the cheesecake immediately if you prefer it creamy, or chill it for 2 hours in the refrigerator for a slightly firmer texture.

Blueberry Coconut Cremeschnitte

Pastry shops in Morocco are filled with *mille-feuille*, a reflection of the strong French influence dating back to the colonial era, when France occupied Moroccan territory for forty-four years. In Switzerland, we have a similar dessert called *cremeschnitte*, also made with layers of pastry and vanilla cream.

Because my favorite *milhojas* (Spain's version of mille-feuille) are made with fruit, I decided to create a twist on the classic, one that would taste and feel different from both the French and Swiss versions.

serves 8

blueberry and peach compote
- 5 ripe peaches, cut into ½-inch (1-cm) slices
- 1½ cups (270 g) sugar or gelling sugar
- 1 teaspoon pectin
- 3 cups (about 500 g) blueberries
- 1 tablespoon lemon juice

coconut whipped ganache
- 1 teaspoon cornstarch (cornflour)
- ¼ cup (60 ml) unsweetened coconut cream
- 1 cup (250 ml) unsweetened coconut milk
- ½ cup (120 ml) plant-based heavy (double) cream
- ¼ teaspoon agar agar or vegan gelatin
- 12½ ounces (350 g) vegan white chocolate, finely chopped

pastry
- 1 package vegan puff pastry (17 × 10-inch/42 × 25-cm rectangle)
- sugar, for sprinkling

assembly
- 1 cup (about 150 g) blueberries
- 2 peaches, cut into cubes
- ½ cup (43 g) unsweetened shredded coconut
- apricot jelly, warmed, for glazing (optional)

method

blueberry and peach compote
In a saucepan, combine the peach slices, sugar, and pectin. Stir well, then warm over medium heat for 5 minutes, until the sugar has dissolved. Add the blueberries and cook for 5–10 minutes, until the fruit are softened but retain their shape. Remove from the heat, stir in the lemon juice, and refrigerate.

coconut whipped ganache
Meanwhile, in a saucepan, mix the cornstarch (cornflour) with the coconut cream until smooth. Whisk in the coconut milk, cream, and agar agar (or vegan gelatin). Cook the mixture over medium heat until bubbles form on the surface and the mixture starts to thicken. Stir continuously to prevent it from burning on the bottom of the pan. Remove from the heat.

Add the white chocolate to the hot mixture and stir until melted. Refrigerate for at least 1 hour.

Once the coconut ganache is cool, whisk it with a hand mixer until smooth and airy. Transfer to a piping bag with a wide nozzle.

pastry
Meanwhile, preheat the oven to 350°F (180°C/Gas Mark 4). Line a baking sheet with parchment (baking) paper.

On a clean work surface, lay out the pastry and cut it in half along the shorter side. Arrange them on the prepared baking sheet and generously sprinkle with sugar. Cover with a layer of parchment (baking) paper, then put a baking sheet on top to weigh down the pastry and make sure it stays flat while baking.

Bake for 10 minutes, or until golden brown and crunchy. Remove from the oven and let cool. Using a serrated knife, cut each half into 12 equal strips (1½ inches/4 cm wide). (We cut it after it bakes to be sure of a clean and straight cut.)

assembly
Lay a piece of the baked pastry on a plate and pipe a layer of the ganache on top. Use a spoon to flatten the ganache a little. Top with a spoonful of the blueberry and peach compote.

Place another piece of pastry on top and repeat the layers of ganache and compote. Top with a third piece of pastry and finish with blueberries, peach pieces, and a sprinkle of shredded coconut. Repeat the process for the remaining portions.

If desired, use a pastry brush to carefully glaze the fruit with the jelly. Let cool.

Fried Crema Catalana Filo Pie

This dessert was first made for an event at KLE celebrating the Catalan region of Girona, and it went down really well. The crunchy, sugary fried crust, with that hit of sharp, sweet fruit and a creamy, spiced centre, makes it hard not to love. We ended up putting it on the à la carte menu at DAR. It's a bit of a mix of Morocco and Catalonia—just like me.

makes 12 pies

crema Catalana

- 1 cup (250 ml) plant-based light (single) cream
- 1 tablespoon cornstarch (cornflour)
- ¼ cup packed (60 g) brown sugar
- 1 strip of orange peel
- 1 strip of lemon peel
- 1 cinnamon stick
- pinch of ground turmeric
- pinch of kala namak black salt
- seeds of 1 vanilla bean
- 1 package filo (phyllo) pastry
- sunflower or vegetable oil, for frying
- Ras el Hanout Sugar (page 258)

variation 1: strawberry fruit salad

- 9 ounces (250 g) strawberries, quartered
- 1 tablespoon muscovado sugar or dark brown sugar
- ½ teaspoon ras el hanout
- pinch of salt

variation 2: citrus salad

- 1 orange, segmented
- 1 blood orange, segmented
- 1 pomelo, segmented
- 2 mint leaves, whole or cut into very thin strips
- 1 tablespoon muscovado sugar or dark brown sugar
- pinch of salt

method

crema Catalana

In a small bowl, whisk 2 tablespoons of the cream with the cornstarch (cornflour) until smooth.

In a saucepan, combine the remaining cream, brown sugar, citrus peels, cinnamon, turmeric, black salt, and vanilla seeds. Warm up over medium-high heat. When hot, add the cornstarch slurry and bring the mixture to a boil. Cook for 2–3 minutes, whisking continuously, until the custard has thickened.

Pour into a container and cover the surface with plastic wrap (clingfilm) to prevent a skin from forming. Cool in the refrigerator for 2 hours, or until set.

Remove and discard the cinnamon stick and citrus peels. Using an immersion blender, blend the custard until smooth.

variation 1: strawberry fruit salad

Combine all the ingredients in a bowl and mix well.

Store in the refrigerator while you prepare the pies.

variation 2: citrus salad

Segment the citrus fruits, removing all membrane and pith. In a bowl, combine all the ingredients and mix well.

Store in the refrigerator while you prepare the pies.

assembly

Place a sheet of parchment (baking) paper on the work surface. Place 5 sheets of filo (phyllo) pastry on top of each other on the parchment (baking) paper, brushing with a little water between each layer. Cut the filo into 4-inch (10-cm) squares. Place a spoonful of crema Catalana in the middle of each square.

Spray the filo with water to help the sheets stick together, then bring together opposite corners of each square to create triangular packages. Pinch along the edges to make sure the packages are well sealed.

Pour the frying oil into a deep saucepan to about 4 inches (10 cm) deep. Heat over medium heat to 350°F (180°C). Fry the filo packages until golden. Transfer to paper towels to drain. Sprinkle with the ras el hanout sugar while still hot.

Serve the filo pies hot with the fruit salad on top.

Chai Buns with Mandarin Labneh

For brunch at DAR, we feature a weekly pastry that changes with the seasons. We regularly bake buns and rolls, but we frequently switch up the fillings and toppings. This recipe is a twist on our cinnamon buns.

The chai spices add depth to the classic cinnamon buns, which are topped with the sweet mandarin labneh.

makes 12 buns

chai butter

- ½ nutmeg, finely grated
- 2 tablespoons ground cinnamon
- 1 tablespoon cardamom pods
- 1 tablespoon cloves
- 2 teaspoons ground ginger
- 2 teaspoons black pepper
- 1 cup (210 g) raw sugar
- pinch of salt
- scant 1 cup (200 g) margarine, room temperature
- 2 tablespoons unsweetened oat milk

mandarin labneh

- 1 cup (225 g) Labneh (page 262)
- zest of 1 mandarin
- 2 tablespoons mandarin juice (about ½ mandarin)
- ½ cup (100 g) raw sugar
- seeds of 1 vanilla bean

buns

- 1⅔ cups (400 ml) unsweetened oat milk
- 2 teaspoons active dry yeast
- 5⅔ cups (700 g) all-purpose (plain) flour
- ¾ cup (150 g) raw sugar
- ⅔ cup (150 g) margarine, cut into cubes
- 1 teaspoon salt
- 1 teaspoon vanilla powder

method

chai butter

Process the spices in a spice grinder to a fine powder.

In a food processor, combine the spice mixture and remaining ingredients. Pulse until well combined. Leave at room temperature.

mandarin labneh

Combine all the ingredients in a bowl. Using an electric handheld whisk, beat until fluffy. Refrigerate.

buns

Mix together the lukewarm milk and dry yeast in the bowl of a stand mixer fitted with the hook attachment. Let sit for 10 minutes while the yeast activates. Add the remaining ingredients and mix together on slow speed for 10 minutes, or until the dough is smooth. Cover the dough with a damp kitchen towel and let rise in a warm place for 2 hours, or until doubled in size.

On a clean, lightly floured surface, roll out the dough into a rectangle, about 19 × 12 inches (48 × 30 cm) and ¼ inch (5 mm) thick. Chill the rolled dough for 10 minutes.

Warm an offset spatula under hot running water, then use it to spread the chai butter evenly over the dough.

Starting on a long edge of the rectangle, roll the dough onto itself to form a log. Chill the dough for 10 minutes. Using a serrated knife, cut it into 12 small or 6 big pieces.

Place the buns on a baking sheet lined with parchment (baking) paper and cover with a damp kitchen towel. Let rise for 1 hour (or overnight in the refrigerator if you want to bake them the next day).

Preheat the oven to 350°F (180°C/Gas Mark 4) and place a lipped baking sheet filled with water on the bottom rack. This will create steam to keep the buns soft and fluffy while they bake.

Using your palm, gently press each bun down in the center to prevent the center from rising too much during baking. Bake in the center of the oven for 40–45 minutes, until golden brown.

Serve warm with a generous spread of the mandarin labneh.

Chef's Note: For extra shiny buns, brush them with milk before and immediately after baking.

Plum Tarts
with Cottage Cheese and Cardamom Syrup

Plum season in Switzerland is short, so every year we order many pounds of plums from local farmers and freeze them to use throughout the year. We bake these tarts for weekend brunch, and they have become a favorite among our regular guests. The caramelized plums balance the creaminess of the cheese, and the cardamom syrup lends a subtle warmth that elevates these tarts from simple to memorable.

---

makes 12 small tarts

filling

2 cups (450 g) Labneh (page 262), Moroccan-Style Ricotta (page 262), or vegan cream cheese
¼ cup (50 g) raw sugar
zest and juice of 1 lemon
pinch of salt
1 teaspoon all-purpose (plain) flour

syrup

scant ½ cup (100 g) margarine
1 tablespoon raw sugar
4 cardamom pods, crushed

assembly

sunflower oil, for greasing
1 package filo (phyllo) pastry
6 fresh or frozen plums, halved
confectioners' (icing) sugar, to finish

method

filling

In a bowl, combine the labneh (or cheese), sugar, lemon zest and juice, and salt. Mix in the flour.

syrup

Melt the margarine in a small saucepan. Stir in the sugar, cardamom, and ¼ cup (60 ml) water. Gently heat until the sugar has dissolved. Strain the syrup through a fine-mesh strainer (sieve).

assembly

Preheat the oven to 350°F (180°C/Gas Mark 4). Grease a muffin pan with a little oil.

Brush the syrup on a sheet of filo (phyllo) pastry. Place another sheet on top and brush with syrup. Repeat until you have used up the pastry or have 6 layers. Cut the filo stack into 6-inch (15-cm) squares. Place a square into each muffin cup, pressing them down in the center so they form small cups. Use a pastry brush to brush the filo with more syrup. Fill each tart with 2 tablespoons of filling.

Place a plum half, cut side up, in each tart and brush with the syrup. If your plums are very large, cut them into slices and arrange the slices on top of the filling.

Bake for 15–20 minutes, until the pastry is golden brown and the plums are soft. Dust with confectioners' (icing) sugar and serve.

Lemon Custard Tart with Mango and Meringue

When I was growing up, we ate only what was sold at small fruit stalls. Shopping at large supermarkets was out of our budget, and we preferred the local produce for sustainability reasons anyway. Mangoes, passion fruit, avocados, and other tropical ingredients made a late appearance in the development of my palate, but are now among my favorites for desserts. Avocados, in particular, works much like butter in pastries and creates super rich custards, as in the milkshake on page 239.

Here, aquafaba—the liquid from cooked or canned chickpeas—steps in as a versatile egg white substitute. It can be whipped into a meringue or emulsified into mayonnaise, making it a staple in vegan baking.

---

serves 8

custard filling

- 1 cup (200 g) raw sugar
- 1 cup (250 ml) plant-based light (single) cream
- ⅓ cup (50 g) cornstarch (cornflour)
- ¼ teaspoon ground turmeric
- zest and juice of 5 lemons (about ¾ cup/200 ml)
- 3½ tablespoons margarine
- pinch of salt
- 2 ripe mangos, peeled and thinly sliced

tart crust

- 1 package store-bought vegan shortcrust pastry
- 3½ tablespoons margarine, melted

meringue

- ¾ cup (90 g) confectioners' (icing) sugar
- ½ cup (120 ml) aquafaba
- 1 teaspoon cream of tartar
- lemon verbena powder or lemon verbena leaves, to finish (optional)

method

tart crust

Preheat the oven to 400°F (200°C/Gas Mark 6). Lightly brush an 11-inch (28-cm) tart pan with melted margarine.

Unroll the dough onto a lightly floured surface. Place the tart pan on top and cut the dough into a circle 2 inches (5 cm) larger than the pan on all sides. Gently line the tart pan with the dough disc, pressing it into the edges. Using a paring knife, trim away any dough that rises above the rim of the pan.

Cut out a 13-inch (32-cm) circle of parchment (baking) paper. Scrunch it up so it's easier to work with, then lay it in the pastry shell (case). Fill the tart with baking beans (pie weights) or rice and bake for 10–15 minutes, until golden brown. Gently lift the paper to remove the weights. Bake the pastry for another 5 minutes, or until golden brown. Let cool for 2 minutes, then remove the tart from the pan and place on a wire rack to cool completely.

custard filling

Mix the sugar, cream, cornstarch (cornflour), turmeric, and lemon zest and juice in a saucepan. Bring to boil over medium heat and simmer for 2 minutes, stirring continuously. Add the margarine and salt. Remove from the heat, then pour the lemon custard into the crust. Cover the surface of the custard with plastic wrap (clingfilm) to prevent a skin from forming. Place in the refrigerator for 1 hour to set.

Arrange the mango slices on top of the custard.

meringue

Using a stand mixer, whisk together the aquafaba, confectioners' (icing) sugar, and cream of tartar for 10 minutes, or until the meringue is smooth, glossy, and the peaks stand upright when you remove the whisk.

Use an offset spatula to spread the meringue on top of the tart. Using a kitchen torch, carefully toast the meringue.

Serve the tart topped with a sprinkle of lemon verbena powder (or fresh lemon verbena leaves), if you like.

Grandma's Cookie Cake

This nostalgic Spanish dessert was something I looked forward to making with my grandmothers, but they both passed before I had the chance. I decided to make it on my own to honour them.

Pastel de galletas is an easy, crowd-pleasing dessert. It is a cookie sheet cake that, typically, children assemble with help from adults—often as a family activity. The assembly involves creating layers of cookies and cream. The cake is then chilled in the refrigerator, ready to be served in the center of the table at dessert time.

Sometimes I alternate the cream with layers of condensed milk or lemon custard. If strawberries are in season, I also love adding them as well. Get creative and make your own version as a family activity.

---

serves 6

custard

- ¼ cup (35 g) cornstarch (cornflour)
- 2 cups (475 ml) plant-based light (single) cream
- ¼ cup (50 g) raw sugar
- seeds of 1 vanilla bean
- pinch of ground turmeric

chocolate milk

- 2 cups (475 ml) unsweetened rice milk
- 2 tablespoons cacao powder, plus extra for dusting

assembly

- 1 cup (250 ml) plant-based heavy (double) cream
- 1½ packages (300 g) plain cookies (biscuits), such as Maria cookies

method

custard

In a bowl, combine the cornstarch (cornflour) and ¼ cup (60 ml) water and stir until smooth.

In a saucepan, combine the cream, sugar, vanilla seeds, and turmeric and bring to a boil. Reduce the heat to medium and whisk in the cornstarch slurry. Whisk for 2 minutes, or until the custard has thickened. Remove from the heat and cover the surface with plastic wrap (clingfilm) to prevent a skin from forming. Refrigerate for at least 2 hours, or until the custard is set.

Once set, blend the custard until smooth. Set aside.

chocolate milk

Combine the milk and cacao powder in a small saucepan and heat over medium heat. Let cool to room temperature.

assembly

Use a hand mixer to whip the cream until stiff. Store in the refrigerator.

Build a station by arranging the Maria cookies (biscuits), chocolate milk, and custard in a row. Spread a spoon of the custard over the bottom and sides of an 8 × 5-inch (20 × 12-cm) baking dish.

One at a time, dip the cookies (biscuits) into the chocolate milk and place in a layer in the baking dish. Spread a spoonful of custard overtop, covering the cookies. Add another layer of cookies dipped in chocolate milk. Repeat this process until the baking dish is full (or the cookies are used up). Cover the top of the cake with a layer of whipped cream. Dust with cacao powder.

Put the cake into the refrigerator for 2 hours to let the cookies soak up all the flavor and for the cake to set.

Serve the cake in the center of the table for everyone to help themselves.

Chef's Note: This soaked cookie cake tastes better the next day, but children are usually impatient. In Venezuela this cake is called *marquesa*, a name adopted during the 17th century after the French name of *marquise au chocolat*.

Jawhara with Cinnamon Custard

This Morocco dessert is my mother's favorite. Every time I prepare it, I feel like I am making it for her, even though we live more than a thousand miles apart. A big part of why I love cooking is the joy of making people happy, spoiling those I care about, and sharing my culture.

Cooking for my mother is no easy task. She is critical, picky, and brutally honest. She doesn't like modern takes or reimagined versions of classic dishes, and she will never eat something just to be polite. So there's definitely pressure to get this recipe just right for her.

---

serves 6

¼ cup (60 g) brown sugar
pinch of gum arabic (aka acacia gum)
3 tablespoons cornstarch (cornflour)
½ teaspoon ground cinnamon
1 cup (250 ml) unsweetened almond milk
1 teaspoon orange blossom water
sunflower oil, for frying
8 sheets brik pastry
2 tablespoons Ras el Hanout Sugar (page 258)
⅔ cup (100 g) raw almonds
salt

method

In a spice grinder, blend the sugar with the gum arabic into a fine powder. In a saucepan, whisk together the sugar mixture, cornstarch (cornflour), and cinnamon. Whisk in the milk. Slowly bring the mixture to a boil over medium heat, stirring continuously. Cook for 2 minutes, or until the custard has thickened. Remove from the heat and whisk in the orange blossom water. Cover with plastic wrap (clingfilm) to prevent a skin forming and let cool in the refrigerator.

Pour the sunflower oil into a wide pan, about 1 inch (2 cm) deep. Heat over medium-low heat to 340°F (170°C). Fry the pastry sheets in double layers in the oil until golden brown. Transfer to a baking sheet lined with paper towel, placing them vertically to drain. Sprinkle the pastry sheets with the ras el hanout sugar.

In the same oil, fry the almonds until golden brown. Transfer to a baking sheet lined with paper towel and sprinkle with salt. Once cool, coarsely chop. Use a food processor or hand blender to blend the chilled custard until smooth.

When ready to serve, place the first double layer of fried pastry on a plate, drizzle with the custard, and top with a quarter of the almonds. Repeat this process for the remaining three layers of pastry. Sprinkle the almonds and ras el hanout sugar overtop and serve immediately.

Almond Baklava

Baklava is often sold from small carts around the medina, the old walled part of many cities in North Africa. While the popular Turkish version is made with pistachios, in Morocco it is more commonly filled with almonds. This baklava has been a staple on the menu at DAR, and we often serve it at special events. The filling is aromatic, nutty, and chewy, thanks to the dates, while the outside layers are flaky and crispy, thanks to the filo (phyllo) pastry.

---

serves 6

syrup

- ⅔ cup (120 g) sugar
- 1 strip lemon peel
- 1 tablespoon lemon juice

filling

- 1¾ cups (250 g) raw almonds
- ½ cup (70 g) dates, pitted (stoned) finely chopped
- 1½ tablespoons maple syrup
- 1 tablespoon margarine, melted
- 1 teaspoon confectioners' (icing) sugar
- 1 teaspoon orange blossom water
- ¼ teaspoon ground cinnamon

assembly

- 12 sheets filo (phyllo) pastry (1 package)
- scant 1 cup (200 g) margarine, melted

to finish

- ¾ cup (100 g) raw almonds, toasted and finely chopped

method

syrup

Combine the sugar and lemon peel in a saucepan. Add ¼ cup (60 ml) water. Heat until the sugar has completely dissolved. Add the lemon juice to avoid crystallization. Set aside to cool.

filling

Preheat the oven to 350°F (180°C/Gas Mark 4). Line a baking sheet with parchment (baking) paper.

Spread the almonds on the prepared baking sheet and toast in the oven until golden brown. Remove from the oven, increasing the temperature to 375°F (190°C/Gas Mark 5).

Finely chop the toasted almonds, then add them to a bowl with the remaining ingredients. Mix well.

assembly

Cut the filo (phyllo) sheets into squares the same size as your baking sheet.

Brush the melted margarine on the bottom of the sheet and place the first sheet of filo on top. Brush the filo sheet with melted margarine and cover with another sheet. Continue in this way until you have used half the pastry.

Spread the filling evenly overtop the filo stack and gently press it into a smooth layer.

Cover the filling with more layers of filo sheets, repeating the process of brushing each sheet with melted margarine until all the pastry has been used.

Use a sharp knife to cut the baklava into 6 squares or the traditional diamond pattern (see picture). Bake for 15 minutes, or until golden and crispy.

to finish

Remove the baklava from the oven and immediately pour the syrup overtop. It should sizzle. Let cool a little, then sprinkle with the toasted almonds. Serve.

Chocolate Coffee Loaf Cake

This is my absolute favorite chocolate cake and the result of extensive testing. Our former pastry chef, Julia Sati, was an exceptional cake decorator, and we developed a "cake bible" together, filled with reliable, well-tested recipes for birthdays, weddings, and other special occasions.

In this recipe, the magic lies in the applesauce and coffee. Both provide moisture while adding just the right touch of bitterness, creating a perfectly rounded, satisfying mouthful of cake.

---

makes 1 large loaf

wet ingredients

1 cup (250 ml) high-protein unsweetened plant milk, such as soy milk
2 tablespoons lemon juice or white vinegar
1 teaspoon chia seeds
1 cup (250 ml) sunflower oil
¾ cup (180 g) unsweetened applesauce
½ cup (120 ml) brewed espresso

dry ingredients

2¼ cups (270 g) all-purpose (plain) flour
1⅔ cups (330 g) raw sugar
1 cup (110 g) cacao powder
1 teaspoon baking powder
1 teaspoon baking soda (bicarbonate of soda)
¼ teaspoon salt
seeds from 1 vanilla bean

peanut butter frosting (icing)

scant ½ cup (100 g) margarine, room temperature
1½ cups (180 g) confectioners' (icing) sugar
seeds from 1 vanilla bean
1 cup (300 g) creamy peanut butter
2 tablespoons plant-based heavy (double) cream

chocolate ganache

½ cup (90 g) vegan chocolate chips
¼ cup (60 ml) plant-based heavy (double) cream
½ teaspoon flaky salt, to finish

method

wet ingredients

Preheat the oven to 350°F (180°C/Gas Mark 4). Line an 11-inch (28-cm) loaf pan with parchment (baking) paper.

Pour the soy milk into a bowl. Make a buttermilk by stirring the lemon juice (or vinegar) into the milk. Set aside for 5 minutes.

Meanwhile, blend the chia seeds into a fine powder. Mix the chia powder with 2 tablespoons water to make a chia "egg." Stir the chia egg into the buttermilk and whisk in the remaining wet ingredients.

dry ingredients

In a large bowl, mix together all the ingredients. Slowly add the wet ingredients to the bowl, whisking until everything is combined.

Pour the batter into the prepared loaf pan. Bake for 40–45 minutes, until a toothpick or skewer inserted in the center of the cake comes out clean. Place the cake on a wire rack to cool while you prepare the toppings.

peanut butter frosting (icing)

Using a hand mixer, beat the margarine with the sugar until softened and fluffy. Add the remaining ingredients and beat together until everything is combined.

chocolate ganache

Melt the chocolate chips in a bowl over a saucepan of boiling water. Stir in the cream.

assembly

Once the cake has cooled, spread the peanut butter frosting (icing) on top. Drizzle over the chocolate ganache. Sprinkle with the flaky salt.

Pandan Chiffon Cake with Kiwi and Strawberries

On one trip to Thailand, I made a point of tasting every pandan cake, fruit roll, and green treat that I could find at bakeries and convenience stores. Pandan is a long, narrow, fragrant green leaf that is wonderful for infusing savory dishes and sweet custards. It has something of a nutty sweet and floral flavor—grassy vanilla might be the best way to describe it. The unique flavor is not easy to substitute. This cake is super fluffy and moist, and every bite takes me right back to Phuket.

makes 1 small cake

wet ingredients

- 4 leaves (¾ oz/25 g) pandan, coarsely chopped
- 1 cup (260 g) soy yogurt
- 3 tablespoons sunflower oil
- 1 tablespoon coconut milk
- 1 teaspoon rice vinegar

dry ingredients

- 1½ cups (180 g) all-purpose (plain) flour
- 1 cup (130 g) confectioners' (icing) sugar
- 1 teaspoon baking powder
- 1 teaspoon baking soda (bicarbonate of soda)
- ¼ teaspoon salt

assembly

- 2 kiwis, sliced
- 5 strawberries, sliced
- ice cream or plant-based heavy (double) cream (optional)

method

wet ingredients

Preheat the oven to 350°F (180°C/Gas Mark 4). Grease a 6-inch (15-cm) angel cake (chiffon) pan.

To make the pandan water, blend the pandan with ½ cup (120 ml) water for 1–2 minutes. Strain the liquid through a fine-mesh strainer (sieve), pressing the pulp with the back of a spoon to release as much of the flavor as possible.

In a large bowl, mix ¼ cup (60 ml) of the pandan water with the remaining wet ingredients.

dry ingredients

Mix together the ingredients. Gradually add the dry ingredients to the wet ingredients, whisking until you have a smooth batter.

assembly

Transfer the batter to the prepared pan and flatten the surface. Bake for 40–45 minutes, until a toothpick or skewer inserted into the center of the cake comes out clean.

Remove the cake from the oven and let cool at room temperature. Once it's cool enough to handle, remove it from the pan and place it on a wire rack to cool completely.

Serve the cake with kiwi and strawberry slices. Top with a scoop of your favorite ice cream (or cream), if you like.

Chef's Note: If you want the fruit to release some of their juices, toss with a pinch of sugar 5 minutes before serving.

Drinks

This chapter is inspired by the non-alcoholic pairings we serve at the restaurants. The team loves creating drinks to complement the menus, adding an extra layer of depth to the dining experience. Some of these recipes are influenced by my travels around the world, while others are rooted in childhood memories.

As a child, I drank Horchata (page 248) and Mediterraneo (page 240) in Spain, but the avocado milkshake was something I encountered only in Morocco, and enjoying one became a ritual when visiting there. I created the rhubarb and concord milkshakes after many trips to South and East Asia, where soy and rice milk are mainstays of the diet.

Concord Grape Milkshake

I used to cook a lot with Concord grapes in New York. They're not available everywhere, but I discovered how popular they were in Japan. They have a distinctive, floral grape flavor.

Milkshakes—especially when made with soy milk—give fruit a whole new dimension. After testing with bananas, pineapples, and many other fruit, Concord grapes proved the most robust, retaining their pungency even when blended with the other ingredients.

serves 8

- 1 cup (250 ml) plant-based heavy (double) cream
- 6 dried fig leaves
- 6½ cups (1.5 liters) unsweetened soy milk
- 1 cup (240 g) granulated sugar
- ½ cup (80 g) Concord grapes
- 1 tablespoon confectioners' (icing) sugar

method

In a small pan, heat the cream with the dried fig leaves. As soon as the cream starts to boil, remove from the heat. Let infuse for 30 minutes. Store in the refrigerator until needed.

Meanwhile, in a blender, blend the milk, sugar, and grapes until smooth and frothy.

Strain the cold infused cream. Using a hand mixer, whip it with the confectioners' (icing) sugar until it thickens and holds its shape in the bowl.

Strain the milkshake through a fine-mesh strainer (sieve). Serve in a tall glass topped with a spoonful of whipped cream.

Strawberry-Orange Blossom Mediterraneo

5 30'

This is an indulgent way to elevate a simple glass of orange juice. In Valencia, where oranges are prized for their juicing quality, this drink is taken to the next level: a generous scoop of vanilla ice cream floats on top. I've added a few extra ingredients here to create an over-the-top version of a "Valenciano" or, as I like to call it, Mediterraneo. The strawberries bring texture, color, and sweetness but also a floral note, which is enhanced by the orange blossom water. Orange blossom water is used to aromatize milk in Morocco, and here it goes especially well with the ice cream.

serves 6

8 ounces (250 g) strawberries, cut into ½-inch (1-cm) cubes
1 teaspoon brown sugar
juice of 20 juicy oranges, such as Valencia (about 5 cups/1.2 liters)
1 tablespoon orange blossom water
1½ quarts (1.4 liters) vanilla or coconut ice cream

method

Place strawberries in a bowl, and sprinkle with the sugar. Mix with a spoon and set aside.

In a pitcher (jug), combine the orange juice and orange blossom water. Pour into tall glasses.

Finish each drink with a scoop of ice cream and a spoonful of the chopped strawberries. Serve with a long spoon and straw.

Rhubarb-White Chocolate Milkshake

5 30'

I absolutely love white chocolate. The one we use at the restaurant is made with coconut and almond instead of milk powder, which makes it even better! This milkshake is definitely for those with a sweet tooth. It would pair well with the KFM Burger (page 188).

The acidity of rhubarb is a good match with the fattiness of the white chocolate. If rhubarb is not available, you can use raspberries instead.

---

serves 8

4 stalks (about 14 oz/400 g) rhubarb, cut into chunks
5 cups (1.2 liters) unsweetened rice milk
7 ounces (200 g) vegan white chocolate, coarsely chopped
ice cubes
⅓ cup (100 g) berry jam

method

In a saucepan, combine rhubarb and milk. Cover with a lid and bring to a boil. Reduce the heat slightly and simmer for 5 minutes, or until the rhubarb is softened. Set aside.

Add the white chocolate to the hot milk mixture. Cover with the lid and let sit for 10 minutes, or until all the chocolate has melted. Blend with a handful of ice cubes until smooth.

Brush the inside of the serving glasses with the berry jam, fill with ice, and pour in the milkshake.

Lychee Ice Tea

We produce all our non-alcoholic drinks, including ice teas, on our drinks menu at the restaurants. This one is a take on the DAR mint ice tea.

I love using gunpowder tea because it's the type of tea used for Moroccan mint tea, but you can easily replace it with green tea.

serves 8

¾ cup (150 g) raw sugar
⅓ cup (25 g) gunpowder tea, rinsed
1 handful mint, plus extra for garnish
juice of 1 lemon
1 (17½-oz/500-g) can lychees

method

Bring 6½ cups (1.5 liters) water to a boil. Add the sugar and gunpowder tea. Remove from the heat and let infuse for 5 minutes. Strain through a fine-mesh strainer (sieve). Add the mint and lemon juice. Refrigerate overnight.

Strain the tea. Serve in tumblers, with 3–4 tablespoons of the liquid from the canned lychees per glass, depending on how sweet you like it. Garnish each glass with 3–4 lychees and a sprig of mint.

Moroccan Avocado-Date Smoothie

(gluten-free) (5)

This popular rich and delicious Moroccan milkshake is available in the streets of the medinas. It is perfect for recharging your energy and guaranteed to deliver a sugar high.

---

serves 8

10 Medjool dates
2 tablespoons golden or sultana raisins
5 cups (1.2 liters) unsweetened almond milk
3 ripe avocados, pitted (stoned) and peeled
pinch of salt
ice cubes

optional
toasted slivered almonds
brigadeiro (page 45)

method

Remove and discard the seeds of the dates. Soak the dates and raisins in the milk for 30 minutes, or until softened.

Put the avocado flesh into a blender along with the milk and soaked fruit, salt, and a handful of ice cubes. Blend to a smooth, creamy consistency.

Serve in tall glasses, topped with toasted slivered almonds and chocolate syrup, if you like.

Pumpkin Horchata

5

Horchata may be a traditional Spanish drink, but its origins trace back to the Phoenician civilization in the Levant. As the Phoenicians expanded across the Mediterranean, they introduced many ingredients, including tiger nuts.

I grew up drinking ice-cold horchata in summer. Walking along the seaside, I preferred it over any ice cream cone. One autumn, we created a pumpkin version of horchata to pair with a dish and it quickly became a favorite.

serves 6

horchata
2 cups (300 g) tiger nuts
2 cinnamon sticks

pumpkin syrup
1 cup (100 g) diced pumpkin
¼ cup (50 g) sugar
½ cinnamon stick

assembly
1 cinnamon stick
ground cinnamon, for garnish

method

horchata
Soak the tiger nuts and cinnamon in 4½ cups (about 1 liter) water for at least 24 hours.

pumpkin syrup
Combine all the ingredients in a saucepan over medium-low heat. Cook for 10 minutes, or until the pumpkin is soft. Discard the cinnamon stick. Transfer the mixture to a blender and blend into a smooth syrup. Strain to remove any lumps. Store in the refrigerator for up to 1 week.

assembly
In a blender, combine the soaked tiger nuts, cinnamon stick and ¼ cup (60 ml) water. Blend for 5 minutes, or until soft. Strain through a very fine-mesh strainer (sieve) or cheesecloth (muslin), squeezing out as much of the liquid out as possible. Stir the pump-kin syrup into the strained liquid. Serve in tumblers, sprinkled with a little ground cinnamon.

Nutmeg Punch

One of my favorite drinks in Malaysia was a nutmeg punch, which was served like a shaken sour cocktail. I loved the spiciness on the nose, the long-lasting taste, and the foamy appearance. Back in Zurich, I created a beverage inspired by that flavor using apple juice, which is both readily available and extremely popular.

serves 8

¼ nutmeg, grated, plus extra for garnish
2 cinnamon sticks, crushed
1 teaspoon cloves, crushed
1 tablespoon chopped fresh ginger
6½ cups (1.5 liters) apple juice
juice of 2 lemons
ice cubes
ground cinnamon, as garnish

method

Toast the spices in a skillet over medium heat for 1–2 minutes, until fragrant. Gently heat the apple juice in a saucepan with the spices and ginger for 5 minutes. Remove from the heat and put in the refrigerator to infuse overnight.

Transfer the infusion to a high speed blender and pulse. Strain through a fine-mesh strainer (sieve) lined with cheesecloth (muslin) or paper towels. Add the lemon juice and shake with ice just before serving.

Strain into tumblers, each with 2 ice cubes. Finish with ground cinnamon.

III

THE PANTRY

Mayos and Aiolis

I have a deep affection for mayonnaise and make no attempt to hide it. It has a remarkable way of elevating even the simplest ingredients. As an emulsion, it carries flavour with exceptional richness and depth. I could easily have devoted an entire book to it, but instead, here are my top ten. They will keep in jars or squeeze bottles in the refrigerator for up to 1 week.

1 Horseradish or Wasabi Mayo

makes 1½ cups (about 350 ml)

- 1½ tablespoons grated horseradish or wasabi paste
- 4 tablespoons aquafaba
- 2 teaspoons lemon juice
- 1 teaspoon ground ginger
- ½ teaspoon salt
- 1 cup (250 ml) sunflower oil

method

In a pitcher (jug), combine the horseradish (or wasabi paste), aquafaba, lemon juice, ginger, and salt. Use an immersion blender to combine. Very slowly add the sunflower oil, blending continuously until the mixture has thickened.

2 Vegan Aioli

makes 1½ cups (about 350 ml)

- 1 clove garlic, crushed
- ¼ cup (60 ml) aquafaba
- 2 teaspoons lemon juice
- ½ teaspoon salt
- 1 cup (250 ml) sunflower oil

method

Bring a small pan of water to boil, then blanch half the crushed garlic for 30 seconds. Drain the garlic and put it into a bowl with the remaining raw garlic, the aquafaba, lemon juice, and salt. Use an immersion blender to combine. Very slowly add the sunflower oil, blending continuously until the mixture has thickened.

3 Harissa Mayo

makes about 1½ cups (350 ml)

- 2 tablespoons aquafaba
- pinch of salt
- ⅔ cup (150 ml) sunflower oil
- ⅓ cup (100 g) plant-based crème fraîche
- ⅓ cup (100 g) harissa paste

method

Put the aquafaba into a pitcher (jug) with a pinch of salt. Very slowly add the sunflower oil, blending continuously with an immersion blender until the mixture has thickened. Stir in the crème fraîche and harissa until well incorporated.

4 Japanese-Style Mayo

makes a 1-pint (475 ml) jar

- 4 tablespoons aquafaba
- 3 tablespoons rice vinegar
- 2 tablespoons soy sauce
- 1 teaspoon Dijon mustard
- 1 tablespoon raw sugar
- 1 teaspoon nutritional yeast
- pinch of salt
- 1½ cups (350 ml) sunflower oil

method

In a small pitcher (jug), use an immersion blender to combine all the ingredients except the oil. Very slowly add the sunflower oil, blending continuously until the mixture had thickened.

5 Mushroom Mayo

makes a 1-pint (475 ml) jar

- 15 g dried mushrooms mix or 1 tablespoon mushroom powder
- 4 tablespoons aquafaba
- 2 tablespoons sweet soy sauce
- 2 tablespoons rice vinegar
- 1 tablespoon Dijon mustard

1¼ cups (300 ml) sunflower oil
pinch of salt

method

Soak the dried mushrooms, if using, in hot water for at least 30 minutes, then drain and finely chop. Put the mushrooms (or mushroom powder) into a pitcher (jug) with the aquafaba, soy sauce, vinegar, and mustard. Use an immersion blender to combine. Very slowly add the sunflower oil, blending continuously until the mixture has thickened. Season with the salt.

6 Miso Mayo

makes 1½ cups (about 350 ml)

4 tablespoons aquafaba
2 tablespoons shiro miso paste
1 tablespoon sweet soy sauce
¼ teaspoon salt
1 cup (250 ml) sunflower oil

method

In a pitcher (jug), use an immersion blender to combine all the ingredients except the oil. Very slowly add the sunflower oil, blending continuously until the mixture has thickened.

7 Ras el Hanout Aioli

makes 1½ cups (about 350 ml)

1 tablespoon ras el hanout
1 quantity Aioli (see above)
2 teaspoons maple syrup

method

In a pan over medium-low heat, gently toast the ras el hanout for 1 minute, or until it releases its aromas. Stir into the aioli along with the maple syrup.

8 Preserved Lemon-Mustard Mayo

makes 1⅔ cups (about 400 ml)

¼ Moroccan preserved lemon
4 tablespoons aquafaba
3 tablespoons Dijon mustard
2½ teaspoons lemon juice
1 cup (250 ml) sunflower oil
salt

method

Remove the seeds from the preserved lemon and finely chop the flesh and peel. Measure out 1 tablespoon and put into a pitcher (jug) with the aquafaba, mustard, and lemon juice. Use an immersion blender to combine. Very slowly add the sunflower oil, blending continuously until the mixture has thickened. Season with salt to taste.

9 Kosho Mayo

makes a 1-pint (475 ml) jar

4 tablespoons aquafaba
2 tablespoons Japanese kosho paste
½ teaspoon salt
zest and juice of 1 lime
1 small bunch cilantro (coriander), finely chopped
1½ cups (350 ml) sunflower oil

method

In a pitcher (jug), use an immersion blender to combine all the ingredients except the oil. Very slowly add the sunflower oil, blending continuously until the mixture has thickened.

10 Dulse Mayo

makes 1⅔ cups (about 400 ml)

1 cup (25 g) dried dulse
¼ cup (60 ml) aquafaba
1 teaspoon salt
juice of 1 lemon
1¼ cups (300 ml) sunflower oil

confit garlic
3 cloves garlic
1 cup (250 ml) sunflower oil

method

Soak the dulse in hot water for at least 30 minutes. Meanwhile, for the confit garlic, put the garlic into a small pan and cover with the sunflower oil. Cook over medium heat until the garlic is lightly browned. Remove from the heat and let cool in the oil.

Drain the dulse, reserving the soaking water. Finely chop the seaweed and put into a pitcher (jug) with the aquafaba, salt, lemon juice, and the cloves of confit garlic. Use an immersion blender to combine. Slowly drizzle in the sunflower oil, blending continuously until the mixture has thickened. Adjust the consistency by blending in a little of the soaking liquid from the dulse.

1
5
2
4
3

6
7
10
8
9

Spice Blends

Having a few glasses of spice blends at home helps me elevate my daily cooking with ease. At the restaurant, we must maintain consistency for our guests, so there's less room for improvisation. But at home, my kitchen becomes a playground where I experiment with flavors that often inspire new dishes on the menu. These blends will keep in airtight containers at room temperature for up to 3 months.

1 Kimchi Togarashi

30'

Use this spice blend as a topping for finished dishes to add some umami. I also like to use it as a seasoning for noodles, rice, vegetables, breads, and mayonnaise.

makes 1¾ cups (200 g)

1 dried citrus peel (about ¾ oz/20 g) (see Note)
1 cup (10 g) dried shiso leaves (see Note)
½ cup (20 g) dried kimchi (see Note)
6 sheets toasted nori
½ cup (70 g) white sesame seeds, toasted
½ cup (70 g) black sesame seeds, toasted

method

Process the citrus peel, shiso leaves, and kimchi in a spice grinder to a fine powder. Add the toasted nori and pulse a few times until it's in small flakes. Stir in the sesame seeds.

Chef's Note:
This recipe works well with a mix of lemon, lime, grapefruit and orange peels. You can easily make the dried citrus peel at home. I like to save the peels each time I make juice. Use a vegetable peeler to remove the skins before you juice any citrus fruits (be careful to take off only the top layer of the skin, avoiding the bitter white pith underneath). Bake the peels on a baking sheet lined with parchment (baking) paper in a 140°F (60°C) oven for at least 3 hours, until completely dry. You can use the same method to dry the shiso leaves and kimchi.

2 Fennel-Cinnamon Sugar

5 30'

Use this flavored sugar in cookies and custards, and to finish cakes. It's also a great addition to a latte.

makes ½ cup (60 g)

4 tablespoons fennel seeds
2 tablespoons ground cinnamon
1 tablespoon cane sugar
1 tablespoon ground lemon verbena

method

Mix everything together in a bowl.

3 Ras el Hanout Sugar

5 30'

Use this flavored sugar for filo (phyllo) pastry desserts, and as a finishing for desserts.

makes 2 cups (180 g)

1 cup (140 g) brown sugar
¼ cup (35 g) ras el hanout
5 tablespoons dried rose petals

method

Mix everything together in a bowl.

4 Chermoula Dry Rub

5 30'

Use this rub for seasoning pickles or salads. Mixed with a bit of oil, it also makes for a great rub for vegetables that will be grilled or pan-fried. You can even sprinkle it over plain rice or couscous to add a burst of flavor.

makes 1½ cups (180 g)

- ½ cup (60 g) ground cumin
- ½ cup (60 g) Moroccan sweet paprika
- ¼ cup (30 g) smoked paprika
- 2 tablespoons salt
- 1 tablespoon black pepper

method

Process all the ingredients together in a spice grinder.

6 Chicory Clove Sugar

Use this flavored sugar to season cakes, cookies, and pastries.

makes 2 cups (250 g)

- 1 cup (200 g) packed brown sugar
- ¼ cup (30 g) chicory coffee powder (see Note)
- 4 cardamom pods
- 1 clove
- 1 nutmeg, grated

method

Process all the ingredients together in a spice grinder.

Chef's Note:
Chicory coffee powder is made from roasted chicory root and is used as a caffeine-free coffee alternative or to deepen coffee flavor. It has a dark, roasted bitterness with subtle caramel notes. It is available from health food stores and well-stocked supermarkets.

6 Spiced Dry Rub

Use this dry rub for grilling vegetables or mixing into vinaigrettes.

makes ½ cup (120 g)

- 3 tablespoons black pepper
- 2 tablespoons ground coriander
- 1 tablespoon mustard powder
- 1 tablespoon brown sugar
- ½ tablespoon ground cumin
- 1 teaspoon salt

method

Process all the ingredients together in a spice blender.

7 Amazigh Spice Blend

Amazigh, the "free people" of North Africa, travel across the region from east to west. As nomads, they are skilled foragers, but they also carry basic ingredients to season the slow-cooked stews they prepare in clay pots over fire beds in the Sahara.

Use as a seasoning for tagines, or mix the spices with some extra-virgin olive oil to make a marinade for grilled vegetables.

makes 2 cups (250 g)

- 1 cup (10 g) dried parsley
- 4 tablespoons sweet paprika
- 4 tablespoons ground cumin
- 3 tablespoons ground turmeric
- 3 tablespoons salt
- 2 tablespoons black pepper
- 2 tablespoons ground ginger
- 2 tablespoons dried garlic powder
- 2 tablespoons muscovado sugar

method

Process all the ingredients together in a spice grinder.

1
2
3
6
4
5

12
1
10
6
8
15
9
11
14
2
3
4
5
13

Refrigerator Staples

The recipes in this chapter are meant to be aces up your sleeve that you can rely on for many occasions. They are easy to make, versatile, and perfect for preparing in larger batches to freeze. You can also customize them with extra flavors to create your own unique variations.

1 Simple Buttermilk

5 30'

This simple recipe comes in handy when baking or battering for frying. You can even use it to make fluffy sponge cakes.

makes 2 cups (475 ml)

- ⅓ cup (75 ml) lemon juice or white vinegar
- 1 cup (250 ml) high-protein unsweetened plant milk, such as soy milk or pea milk

method

Mix the lemon juice (or vinegar) into the milk, stirring well. Let sit for 10 minutes. Refrigerate until needed.

You can store the buttermilk in an airtight container in the refrigerator for up to 3 days, but I recommend making it fresh every time you need it.

2 Traditional Labneh

5

From the countries of Levant, this rich and indulgent strained yogurt will become an essential.

makes 3 cups (750 g)

- 4 cups (1 kg) soy yogurt
- ½ teaspoon salt

method

Mix the yogurt and salt together. Hang the mixture in cheesecloth (muslin) set over a bowl in the refrigerator for 24–36 hours. Putting a weight on top to press the cheese will speed up the draining process.

For a lighter version, whip the mixture with an electric handheld whisk to incorporate some air.

3 Labneh

5

This vegan labneh is a perfect substitute for cream cheese, heavy (double) cream, or yogurt.

makes 3 cups (750 g)

- 2 cups (500 g) soy yogurt
- 2 cups (500 g) soy crème fraîche
- juice of 1 lemon
- ¼ teaspoon salt

method

Mix all the ingredients together. Hang the mixture in cheesecloth (muslin) set over a bowl in the refrigerator for 24–36 hours.

For a lighter version, whip the mixture with an electric handheld whisk to incorporate some air. I recommend cooking the labneh fresh every week. If you freeze it, whisk or blend it before using.

4 Moroccan-Style Ricotta

This ricotta is known as *jben* in Morocco and is sold wrapped in palm leaves, the farmers going from door to door in the mornings to sell the fresh batch. Here are two recipes to make at home.

makes 2 cups (500 g)

- 4 cups (1 liter) unsweetened soy milk (see Note)
- 1 teaspoon dried oregano
- juice of 2 lemons

seasoning

- ¼ teaspoon salt
- ¼ teaspoon black pepper
- 1 teaspoon lemon juice
- extra-virgin olive oil, for drizzling (optional)

method

In a saucepan, heat the milk with the oregano over medium heat. Once the milk starts to simmer, remove it from the heat. Immediately add the lemon juice and gently stir twice. Let the milk sit in the pan undisturbed for 30 minutes. Strain through a sieve lined with cheesecloth (muslin). Store in the refrigerator set over a bowl for at least 2 hours. The cheese will become thick and creamy.

Once ready, season the ricotta in a bowl with the salt, pepper, and lemon juice. For a more Mediterranean flavor, add a drizzle of olive oil as well.

Serving option: Blend the ricotta with an immersion blender until smooth. It can then easily spread onto toast.

Store in an airtight container in the refrigerator for up to 5 days.

Chef's note:
For a richer cheese, replace half the soy milk with soy buttermilk (page 262).

5 Soft Cheese

This creamy cheese can simply be spread on toast with Apple Honey (page 265) or used in cakes, tarts, and sauces.

makes 3 cups (750 g)

- 2 cups (475 ml) unsweetened soy milk
- ¼ teaspoon salt
- ¼ teaspoon dried thyme
- 2 cups (475 ml) soy buttermilk (page 262)

method

In a saucepan, bring the milk with the salt and thyme to a simmer over medium-low heat. Remove from the heat, pour in the buttermilk, and gently stir twice. Let sit for 30 minutes. Strain through a sieve lined with cheesecloth (muslin). Refrigerate for at least 2 hours and up to 24 hours. The longer the cheese drains, the thicker and firmer it will be.

Store in an airtight container in the refrigerator for up to 5 days.

6 Feta-Style Cheese

I love a sour, tangy, and salty crumb topping on pasta, salad, tartines, dips ... and this recipe checks all the boxes. I particularly love eating it with crushed fennel seeds, toasted almonds, and a drizzle of apple honey on crackers. It has a long shelf life.

makes 3½ cups (800 g)

- ¾ cup (150 g) refined coconut oil, melted
- 1 pound (500 g) medium-firm tofu, room temperature
- juice of 1 lemon
- 3 tablespoons apple cider vinegar
- 2½ tablespoons nutritional yeast
- 2 teaspoons onion powder
- 2 teaspoons garlic powder
- 2 teaspoons salt
- ¼ teaspoon dried dill
- ¼ teaspoon dried thyme

method

Put all the ingredients into a blender and blend for 5 minutes, or until smooth and creamy. Transfer to a shallow baking dish. Let cool in the refrigerator for at least 4 hours, until firm.

For a whipped "feta" that can be piped or easily spread, add ½ cup (120 ml) water to a bowl with the chilled cheese and mix with an immersion blender until all the water is incorporated.

Store in the refrigerator for up to 2 weeks, or in the freezer for 3 months.

7 Chermoula Marinade

30'

Chermoula is the go-to marinade in Morocco: a spoonful of chermoula is a spoonful of the flavor of Morocco. Use it as a marinade for roasted vegetables such as cauliflower or eggplant (aubergine).

makes 1½ cups (about 300 g)

chermoula marinade

- 5 cloves garlic
- ½ cup (120 ml) lemon juice (about 3 lemons)
- 4 tablespoons extra-virgin olive oil
- 4 tablespoons Moroccan sweet paprika
- 4 tablespoons ground cumin
- 2 tablespoons smoked paprika
- 1 teaspoon black pepper
- 1½ teaspoons salt
- 1 large handful parsley, finely chopped
- 1 large handful cilantro (coriander), finely chopped

method

chermoula marinade
In a blender, blend all the ingredients except the parsley and cilantro (coriander) until well combined. Stir in the chopped fresh herbs by hand. Store in an airtight container in the refrigerator for up to 2 weeks, or in the freezer for up to 2 months.

Chef's note:
To make chermoula oil, mix 1 quantity of chermoula marinade with 3 cups (750 ml) extra-virgin olive oil. Drizzle over scrambled tofu or dips.

8 Preserved Lemon-Chili Oil

30'

This oil is delicious drizzled on flatbreads or over roasted vegetables.

makes 1 cup (about 250 ml)

- 1½ piece preserved salted lemon, finely diced peel
- 1 red chile, finely sliced
- 1 tablespoon chopped mint
- 2 tablespoons chopped cilantro (coriander)
- 1 teaspoon ground pink peppercorns
- ¼ teaspoon salt
- ¾ cup (175 ml) extra-virgin olive oil
- 1 lemon

method

Put the preserved lemon peel, chiles, mint, and cilantro (coriander) in a bowl. Add the pink pepper, salt, and then the olive oil, mixing well. Add a squeeze of lemon juice just before serving. I recommend using this oil fresh, but it will keep in the refrigerator for up to 2 days.

10 Onion Bechamel

This onion bechamel can be used in many dishes, including lasagna and baked pasta dishes, or on top of white asparagus. You can also make a thicker version as a filling for *croquetas* by adding an extra tablespoon of all-purpose (plain) flour to the onions.

makes a 1-pint (475 ml) jar

- 3½ tablespoons margarine
- 3–4 onions, finely diced
- 4 cups (1 liter) unsweetened oat milk
- 2 teaspoons grated nutmeg
- 2 teaspoons salt
- ½ teaspoon black pepper
- ½ cup (60 g) all-purpose (plain) flour

method

Heat the margarine in a large skillet over medium-low heat. Add the onions and sweat until softened and translucent.

Meanwhile, heat the milk in a saucepan. Season with the nutmeg, salt, and pepper.

Once the onions are softened, add the flour and cook for 1 minute, whisking regularly to prevent the flour from sticking to the pan.

Slowly add ladlefuls of the warm milk to the onions, whisking continuously to achieve a creamy sauce without any lumps of flour. Once all the milk is incorporated, simmer for 1–2 minutes to let the sauce thicken.

Store in an airtight container in the refrigerator for up to 1 week, or in the freezer for up to 3 months.

11 XO Mushroom Sauce

When I am very tired, I love eating a bowl of sushi rice with a big spoon of this amazing XO sauce. Give it a try!

makes a 1-pint (475 ml) jar

base

- 2 small white onions (7 oz/200 g), finely chopped
- 1 tablespoon sunflower oil
- pinch of salt
- 1 pound (500 g) button mushrooms, finely chopped
- 2 tablespoons mushroom oyster sauce

seasoning

- ⅓ cup (50 g) sesame seeds
- 3 red chiles, finely chopped
- 2 bay leaves
- 1 small handful cilantro (coriander), finely chopped
- 1 tablespoon chili powder
- 1 teaspoon salt
- 1 teaspoon sugar
- 1 star anise
- ½ teaspoon black pepper
- 1 cup (250 ml) sunflower oil

optional

- soy sauce
- maple syrup
- Szechuan pepper

method

In a skillet over medium heat, sweat the onions in the sunflower oil with the salt until translucent. Add the mushrooms and continue to cook, stirring occasionally, until the mixture is golden brown. Stir in the mushroom oyster sauce.

In a stainless-steel bowl, combine the sesame seeds, chiles, bay leaves, cilantro (coriander), chili powder, salt, and sugar. Lightly toast the star anise and black pepper in a pan for 1–2 minutes, until fragrant. Add the star anise and pepper to the bowl and mix well. Set aside.

In a saucepan, heat the sunflower oil to 340°F (170°C). Pour it over the ingredients in the bowl and carefully stir everything together.

Transfer the mixture to the mushroom skillet and cook over low heat for at least 30 minutes, until dark brown but not burned.

Taste and season with soy sauce or maple syrup, if you like. I also like to add Szechuan pepper.

Store the sauce in a glass jar, covered with the frying oil, in the refrigerator for up to 2 months. Stir before using.

12 Hand-Shaped Pasta

Plant-based pasta is deceptively easy to make. You can make a bigger batch to store in the freezer for up 3 months, then cook it from frozen; just remember to add an extra minute to the cooking time.

serves 4

- 2¼ cups (400 g) fine semolina
- ¾ cup (100 g) all-purpose (plain) flour
- ½ teaspoon salt
- 1½ tablespoons extra-virgin olive oil

method

Put the semolina, flour, and salt in a food processor and mix. Slowly add 1 cup (250 ml) cold water and the olive oil until a dough with large crumbs forms and almost comes together into a ball.

Remove the dough and knead it for 3 minutes, or until it holds together in a smooth ball. Transfer to an airtight container and let rest for 30 minutes (or for up to 24 hours in the refrigerator).

Roll out the dough and shape the pasta as you like. Once shaped, the pasta can be dried, frozen, or immediately cooked in salted water to al dente.

13 Apple Honey

A plant-based floral honey can give a special touch to a dish. While not essential, fresh seasonal edible flowers make it outstanding.

makes 1½ cups (about 400 g)

- 2 cups (500 g) apple juice
- 1½ cups (320 g) sugar
- 2 tablespoons chamomile tea leaves
- ½ teaspoon fennel seeds
- 2 tablespoons lemon juice

method

In a saucepan, gently heat the apple juice and sugar over low heat until the sugar has completely dissolved. Remove from the heat and add the chamomile and fennel seeds. Cover with a lid and let infuse for at least 30 minutes.

Strain the infusion into a saucepan. Warm over medium-high heat to 235°F (110°C). Remove from the heat and whisk in the lemon juice. If fresh flowers are in season, add them at this stage and let infuse for 30 minutes before straining. The consistency will be honey-like.

Store in a glass jar at room temperature, just like regular honey.

14 Hot Honey

Sweet and spicy is a match made in heaven. Drizzle it on pizzas, tartines, ice cream, and pasta dishes, and even cocktails.

makes 1 cup (250 ml)

- 1 cup (300 g) Apple Honey (see above)
- 2 teaspoons Espelette or cayenne pepper
- 2 tablespoons apple cider vinegar

method

In a saucepan, gently warm the honey and pepper over low heat. Remove from the heat and let cool before stirring in the vinegar.

Store in a glass jar in the refrigerator for up to 2 months.

15 "Bacon Jam but It's Rice"

Smoky, chewy, salty bites can improve any dish. Use this version as little pops of flavor in salads, stir fries, or a scramble.

makes 1 cup (250 ml)

- ⅓ cup (75 g) sushi rice
- ⅓ cup (75 ml) gluten-free tamari or soy sauce
- 2½ tablespoons nutritional yeast
- 2 tablespoons maple syrup
- 1 tablespoon extra-virgin olive oil
- 1 tablespoon gluten-free BBQ sauce
- ½ teaspoon sweet paprika
- ½ teaspoon garlic powder
- pinch of salt
- pinch of kala namak black salt
- ¼ teaspoon liquid smoke
- sunflower oil, for frying

method

Rinse the rice in a sieve for 5 minutes, or until the water runs clear. Cook the rice.

Using a rice cooker, mix the rice with all the remaining ingredients. Add 1 cup (250 ml) water and cook until the rice is soft and almost overcooked. Place the rice in a bowl and let stand, uncovered overnight in the refrigerator.

Heat a drizzle of oil in a non-stick skillet over medium heat. Add the rice and fry for 5 minutes until crispy on the outside.

Store in an airtight container in the refrigerator for up to 3 days, or for up 2 months in the freezer.

INDEX

Page numbers in *italics* refer to illustrations

V

W

X

Y

Z

ACKNOWLEDGMENTS

Thank you to my restaurant teams for making every day an opportunity for change and for handling the chaos of all my open projects so gracefully. You are all stars!

Thank you to my executive editor, Emily Takoudes, for trusting me throughout this process and guiding me through the incredible opportunity of writing a Phaidon book. A dream come true for any chef.

Thank you to the entire Phaidon team, including my editor, Michelle Meade, for taking the time to answer all my questions and for polishing every detail of this book with such love and respect.

I am grateful to Erna Drion for capturing through her lenses since day one not only the recipes of this book but also the spirit of everything we do at the restaurants. Thankful to have Dasha Tovstenko bring structure and organization to the photo shoot; we would have suffered without you.

Thank you to chefs Alessandro Scaccia and Emily Barrat, my kitchen dream team, for your unconditional support and invaluable input in making these recipes the best they can be.

And finally, thank you to my family and to my compassionate husband, Marc Barrafon, for your patience as I spent so many of our weekends and holidays writing and rereading this manuscript.

ABOUT THE AUTHOR

Zineb Hattab was born in Spain to Moroccan parents and originally trained as an industrial engineer. The precision of that early career shaped the discipline she later brought to the kitchen, where she found a more instinctive calling: creating food that connects, nourishes, and reflects her cultural roots.

Her culinary path led through acclaimed kitchens, including El Celler de Can Roca, Osteria Francescana, and Cosme, where she refined her technique and deepened her commitment to craft. In 2020, she opened KLE in Zurich, a completely plant-based fine dining restaurant blending Mediterranean warmth, North African depth, and global sustainability. Within two years, it earned both a red and green Michelin Star, a first for vegan cuisine in Switzerland. She followed with DAR, a second plant-based restaurant rooted in her heritage and also recognized with a green Michelin Star.

Beyond her restaurants, Zizi is an advocate for sustainability, inclusion, and equitable food systems. She shares her perspective through international teaching and speaking, and through her cookbook *Taste of Love*, which captures her belief that plant-based cooking carries both cultural meaning and creative possibility.

Recipe Notes

Unless otherwise specified:

- All spices are freshly ground.
- Individual vegetables and fruit, such as carrots and apples, are assumed to be medium.
- Plant-based light (single) cream is 15% fat.
- Plant-based heavy (double) cream is 33% fat.
- All sugar is superfine (caster) sugar and all brown sugar is cane or turbinado (demerara).
- All salt is fine sea salt.
- All pepper is black and freshly ground.
- Round cake pans are assumed to be springform.

Cooking times are for guidance only, because individual ovens vary. If using a conventional oven, follow the manufacturer's directions concerning oven temperatures.

Exercise a high level of caution when following recipes involving any potentially hazardous activity, including the use of high temperatures, open flames, and when deep-frying. In particular, when deep-frying, add food carefully to avoid splashing, wear long sleeves, and never leave the pan unattended.

Some recipes include raw or very lightly cooked fermented products. These should be avoided by the elderly, infants, pregnant people, convalescents, and anyone with an impaired immune system.

As some species of mushrooms have been known to cause allergic reaction and illness, do take extra care when cooking and eating mushrooms and do seek immediate medical help if you experience a reaction after preparing or eating them.

Exercise caution when making fermented products, ensuring all equipment is spotlessly clean, and seek expert advice if in any doubt.

When no quantity is specified, for example of oils, and sugars used for finishing dishes or for deep-frying, quantities are discretionary and flexible.

All herbs, shoots, flowers, and leaves should be picked fresh from a clean source.

Do exercise caution when foraging for ingredients, which should only be eaten if an expert has deemed them safe to eat. In particular, do not gather wild mushrooms yourself before seeking the advice of an expert who has confirmed their suitability for human consumption.

Both metric and imperial measures are used in this book. Follow one set of measurements throughout, not a mixture, as they are not interchangeable.

All spoon and cup measurements are level, unless otherwise stated. 1 teaspoon = 5 ml; 1 tablespoon = 15 ml.

Australian standard tablespoons are 20 ml, so Australian readers are advised to use 3 teaspoons in place of 1 tablespoon when measuring small quantities.

Phaidon Press Limited
2 Cooperage Yard
London
E15 2QR

Phaidon Press Inc.
111 Broadway
New York, NY 10006

Phaidon SARL
55, rue Traversière
75012 Paris

phaidon.com

First published 2026

ISBN 978 1 83729 262 2

A CIP catalogue record for this book is available from the British Library and the Library of Congress.

Commissioning Editor: Emily Takoudes
Project Editor: Michelle Meade
Production Controller: Andie Trainer
Design: Balmer Hählen
Photography: Erna Drion

Printed in China

Phaidon would like to thank Priscilla Balmer, Theresa Bebbington, Ruth Ellis, Yvo Hählen, Julia Hasting, João Mota, Judy Phillips, Faye Robinson, Ellie Smith, Tracey Smith, Daria Tovstenko, and Jonas Wanstock.